SLIM WOK
COOKERY

Ceil Dyer

ANOTHER BEST-SELLING VOLUME FROM HPBooks®

Publisher: Rick Bailey; Executive Editor: Randy Summerlin;
Editorial Director: Elaine R. Woodard
Art Director: Don Burton; Book Design: Paul Fitzgerald
Typography: Cindy Coatsworth, Michelle Carter
Director of Manufacturing: Anthony B. Narducci
Food Stylist: Susan Zechmann; Photography: Cy DeCosse Inc.

Published by HPBooks, Inc.
P.O. Box 5367, Tucson AZ 85703   602/888-2150
ISBN 0-89586-412-6
Library of Congress Catalog Card Number 86-80026
© 1986 HPBooks, Inc.   Printed in the U.S.A.
1st Printing

Cover Photo: Sole with Potatoes & Asparagus, page 87.

CONTENTS

Ceil Dyer

A graduate of Louisiana State University, Ceil was a New York food publicist with wine and food companies for a number of years. Later she wrote a column featuring quick gourmet recipes for entertaining. Now, away from the hustle of New York City, Ceil Dyer resides in a quiet resort area on the east coast. In her fashionable condominium, she spends much of her time developing new and exciting recipes. She especially likes those that help her watch her weight but still have the taste of gourmet food. Ceil uses her wok every day, whether for her own meals or entertaining family and friends.

A prolific writer, Ceil has authored more than 30 cookbooks including bestseller *Wok Cookery, More Wok Cookery* and *Chicken Cookery*, published by HPBooks.

INTRODUCTION

Weight reduction or just plain losing unwanted pounds is a major concern for many people today. Most everyone is aware that the only sure, healthful way to lose weight is to reduce the number of calories you take in, increase the number of calories you burn each day through exercise, or a combination of both. It is also important to modify your eating pattern to help maintain your desired weight for life.

Wok cooking techniques are of prime importance in Oriental cooking. By using some of the traditional Oriental cooking methods, such as stir-frying, steaming or poaching, calories can be reduced and you can still enjoy great-tasting food. Quick-to-prepare, stir-fried dishes with meat, poultry or fish and vegetables or rice add up to low-calorie, flavorful meals. Poaching and steaming reduce calories in recipes because they eliminate the need for added oil. In other stir-fry recipes, oil has been cut to a minimum to reduce calories.

Slim Wok is for the person who enjoys great food, but wants to lose weight. Foods cooked in a wok help to cut calories without sacrificing flavor, nutrients or real appetite satisfaction. *Slim Wok* has recipes that will satisfy both your appetite and your longing for great-tasting food.

Each recipe in this book has been tested. Calorie counts were established through a reputable nutritional data base. All recipes are portion-controlled with a calorie count not to exceed 350 per serving. Garnishes or optional ingredients were not included in calorie counts. Ingredients giving a range of equivalence were calculated in the larger amount.

No matter what type of meal you are preparing, wok cooking can work for you. Ingredients used are low in fat and high in complex carbohydrates. They include fresh vegetables, rice, noodles, fish, poultry and lean meats. Ingredients are also high in vitamins, minerals, protein, starch and fiber. Together they are satisfying and nutritionally sound.

It is always fun to prepare food in a wok. No other cooking method has so many possibilities. Serving and eating wok-cooked foods is just as delightful. The bright color and crisp texture of stir-fried dishes along with the elegance and enticing aroma are enough to win over both family and friends.

This is a book filled with delicious recipes you can savor while counting calories. Go ahead—get out your wok and try this international array of recipes. And, best of all, enjoy losing weight at the same time.

Cutting Techniques for Stir-Frying

The short cooking time typical of most stir-fry dishes is made possible by the way raw ingredients are sliced, diced, minced or chopped. With proper cutting, foods can be brought close to tenderness before going into the wok. The characteristics of each ingredient determine the method of cutting.

The major ingredients in a stir-fry dish are generally cut to the same size and shape so they will cook quickly and all be ready to eat at the same time. They are also cut with a critical eye for appearance. The dish should not only taste good but also look appetizing!

Here are a few tips on preparing vegetables for wok cooking:

To mince garlic: Place a garlic clove on a cutting board. Press down firmly with the flat side of a cleaver until peel separates and garlic is slightly crushed. Pull off and discard peel. Holding the tip of the cleaver on the chopping board, cut garlic horizontally, then vertically into a small dice. Push together and chop until finely minced and pieces will hold together when rolled into a ball.

To chop onions: Remove and discard peel. Cut in half from top to bottom. Place cut-side down on chopping board; cut across first vertically, then horizontally.

To cut bell pepper into strips: Remove and discard rounded ends or save for other use. Cut each pepper in half from top to bottom. Remove and discard seeds and white pith. Quarter pepper; then cut quarters lengthwise into 1/4-inch-wide strips.

To slice mushrooms: Cut off and discard stem ends. One at a time, hold each mushroom under cold running water; rub mushroom clean with your fingers. Then blot dry with paper towels. If mushrooms are left standing in water, they will absorb moisture and lose flavor. Cut across into thin T-shapes. Quarter large whole mushrooms or chop, dice or mince following recipe directions.

To slice celery: Remove leafy end pieces and save for other use. Remove and discard tough ends. Peel off tough strings. Place celery on its side on a chopping board. Cut across at a 45-degree angle into thin crescent-shaped slices.

Dice—Cut in thin slices; stack slices and cut across them in fine strips. Then cut strips across and dice.

Thin Slicing—Cut through vegetables to show direction of grain. This is the best way to slice fresh mushrooms.

To slice zucchini or yellow squash: Trim off and discard end pieces; do not peel. Rinse briefly under cold water. With a sharp, small knife, scrape off any damaged skin. Cut at a 45-degree angle into thin oval slices.

To prepare other firm round or cylindrical vegetables: Remove and discard peel, if necessary. If large, cut in half lengthwise. Cut lengthwise again through center of each half, then cut into slices of the same width; separate into pie-shaped wedges. Or, cut in half and place cut-side down on a chopping board. Cut across first vertically, then horizontally into small dice.

To cut green onion: Cut off root end and most of the green tops. Reserve tops to slice or chop for garnish, if desired. Remove and discard first layer of skin. Cut across onion into thin slices.

Dice in Cubes—First cut across, then line up and cut checkerboard fashion in fine cubes.

Diagonal Slicing—Less-tender meats and fibrous vegetables are cut diagonally to tenderize them. The difference between this and straight-across slicing is the knife is held at an angle to the food. This produces thin slices for fast cooking.

Pie-Slice Sections—Cut vegetables in half lengthwise. Cut through center of each half. Then cut in slices the same width. Separate into pie-shaped wedges.

Matchstick-Thin Strips—Cut in thin slices; then stack slices and cut in thin strips.

Thinly Sliced Meat—Freeze meat until very firm. Using a sharp knife, slice across grain as thinly as possible.

Diamond Shapes—Roll long vegetables, such as green onions, celery or carrots, as you make diagonal cuts.

Carrot Flowers—Peel carrot; then cut V-shaped wedges lengthwise, spacing equally all around carrot. Cut in 1/8-inch-thick slices resulting in flowers.

Cleaning & Caring for Your Wok

The wok is the traditional Oriental cooking utensil. It can be used to cook almost any food or to cook several foods at the same time. It gives you more surface on which to cook foods than almost any other utensil. The shape distributes heat evenly so there are no hot spots on its surface. Because of the wide top, it is easy to stir and blend foods.

Woks come in a range of sizes from 2- to 6-quart capacity. If you do lots of entertaining, the larger wok will make meal preparation easier. For most individuals and families, the 3-quart capacity is sufficient.

All woks have the same basic bowl-shape. Most come with a dome lid that is essential when steaming. Wok handles and lid knobs may be metal, heat-resistant plastic, wood or wood-covered metal. Woks with rounded bottoms have a separate metal ring base. Woks with flat bottoms can be placed directly on a stove burner. Electric woks have temperature controls that can be set for any temperature you desire.

Your wok may come with a steamer rack, an Oriental-style spatula and a spoon for stir-frying. If these tools did not come with your wok, they can be purchased separately or you can use wooden spoons or metal slotted spoons you already have.

A wok is one of the simplest utensils to use and clean. Before using a wok, it should be seasoned. Here is an easy method for cleaning and seasoning a rolled-steel non-electric wok. First, remove the machine-oil coating applied by the manufacturer to prevent rust. Immerse the wok in hot soapy water and soak about an hour. Add boiling water once or twice to keep water hot. Drain wok; clean inside and out with a scouring pad to remove all machine oil. Rinse well with hot water. Dry wok on a wok ring over a burner set at medium heat. With the burner still on, pour in 1 to 2 teaspoons peanut oil or vegetable oil other than corn oil. Corn oil flames at a lower temperature than other oils. Rub oil into wok surface with clean paper towels. Repeat oiling and rubbing two or three times. Wipe with a clean paper towel. Now you have seasoned your wok.

You can clean your wok easily with hot soapy water.

After your wok is dry, add 1 teaspoon oil. Rub it over the inside with a paper towel.

To clean your wok after cooking, simply wash with hot soapy water. Rinse well and place over medium heat to dry. Rub 1 teaspoon oil onto the surface with paper towels.

If your wok is electric, seasoning and cleaning are equally easy. Always remove heat control before starting to clean your wok. To season your electric wok, soak it as you would the conventional type. Do not use scouring pads on the non-stick interior. Dry thoroughly, especially the heat-control socket. Rub cooking surface with 2 teaspoons oil. Now your electric wok is ready to use.

To clean an electric wok, first detach heat control. Wash in hot soapy water. If stubborn foods stick, try a plastic-type scrubbing pad. The wok may look clean but tiny food particles may adhere to the non-stick finish and must be removed. Dry thoroughly and rub interior with 1 teaspoon oil. Be sure the heat-control socket is completely dry before reinserting heat control.

Conventional steel woks with a non-stick interior finish are seasoned and cleaned just like an electric one.

Cleaning wok accessories is even easier. Your wok may be purchased as a set, complete with a tall lid and a rack for steaming as well as a perforated-metal ring to hold the wok securely over the stove burner, or these may be purchased separately. They require no special cleaning. The rack and ring can go in the dishwasher if desired and the aluminum steaming lid is simply washed in hot soapy water, rinsed and dried. Don't wash the lid in the dishwasher because the drying heat can ruin wooden or plastic knobs.

Store your wok on the kitchen counter. It's decorative and handy, but most importantly, it stays fresh and ready to use. Any oil will become rancid if stored in a dark warm place for a prolonged period and your wok has been seasoned with oil.

Slim Wok Cooking Techniques

A wok is an all-purpose cooking pot that is especially great for preparing low-calorie foods. It has a rounded shape and high, sloping sides in which you will need less oil than for traditional frying. By eliminating 1 tablespoon oil from a recipe, you immediately cut about 125 calories from the prepared dish. When seasoned correctly, a wok becomes a non-stick pot. The surface will not scratch if handled correctly and will last a lifetime. The wok can then be used to stir-fry vegetables or cook meats, fish and poultry without added oil or fat of any kind. Because of the size and shape of a wok, it can also be used as a steamer, holding more food in one layer at a time than most other steamers. Steamed foods can add variety to the dieter's collection of low-calorie, quick-cooking but extremely nutritious and flavorful foods.

STIR-FRYING

Stir-frying is the most popular and best-known method used in wok cookery. It is a basic cooking process using high heat, shallow oil and constant stirring. It results in quick cooking of cut-up ingredients. Sometimes it is misunderstood by the Western cook who confuses it with sautéing. When food is sautéed, it is stirred in hot butter, oil or other fat over medium-high heat.

To stir-fry, food is cut into small, uniform pieces. Meats for stir-frying are usually ground or cut in thin strips. Vegetables, such as carrots, onions and green peppers, are diced or cut in thin slices. Leafy vegetables, such as spinach or lettuce, are shredded or torn into bite-sized pieces.

The wok is heated over high heat and a small amount of oil is added, if needed, to keep the food from sticking. Peanut oil is used for wok cooking and for good reason. This oil can be brought to a high temperature without smoking and its bland flavor doesn't overpower other ingredients. Never substitute solid shortening, butter or margarine for the oil.

Once the oil is very hot, the food is added as directed in the recipe. Then an action similar to turning and tossing begins. The food is cooked only until it begins to look and taste cooked. Vegetables should retain their bright colors and crisp texture. When cooked, meat is no longer red, chicken turns white and firm, and fish is firm and opaque through the center.

A key to stir-frying success is to have all the ingredients ready *before* you begin. Cooking time is very short and there is simply no chance to stop and look for ingredients.

STIR-STEAMING IN A DRY WOK

Prepare vegetables as directed in the recipe. Place wok directly over high heat. Do not use round metal ring holder. When a few drops of water flicked into the bottom of the dry wok sizzle and evaporate immediately, the wok is ready.

Add prepared vegetables; immediately begin to stir-fry, tossing vegetables up against the side of the wok and letting them fall back to the center as you stir and turn them. This action is similar to tossing a salad. When vegetables are slightly moistened by their own juices, sprinkle with 1 to 2 tablespoons broth, water or other liquid. Cover and steam vegetables 30 seconds. Continue to stir-fry until vegetables are crisp-tender or cooked to desired doneness. Season as desired and serve.

Foods to be stir-fried should be sliced, diced or otherwise cut to ensure fast cooking.

STEAMING

Steaming is the most subtle form of wok cookery. Vegetables and meats as well as custards and desserts can be steamed in a wok. This method cooks by moist hot air instead of dry heat. Steamed foods retain their moisture, natural color and fresh flavor. Steam foods only until slightly tender; don't overcook. Foods can also be wrapped in foil or paper to cook. Steamed vegetables are bright in color, and cooked until their crispy tenderness is just right. Custards are delicate yet firm, and cakes are moist and delicious.

Woks are usually sold with a high domed lid that will allow the hot moist air to circulate around the food as it cooks. The steamer rack generally provided with your wok is usually no more than two flat wooden bars that have been criss-crossed to fit into the wok. To steam, you will also need either an Oriental-style flat bamboo steamer or a metal rack. If you do not have either piece of equipment, a 9-inch round cake rack or a rack about 2 inches smaller in circumference than your wok lid can be substituted.

To steam, pour water into wok to 1 inch below rack. Place wok over medium heat; bring water to a simmer. This will produce steam but the water won't boil up into the food. Place food directly on the rack or in a shallow heat-proof dish on the rack. Cover and begin timing. It's best to watch the timing and be careful not to overcook foods. Steamed fish takes only minutes to reach perfection. Follow the times given in the recipes or vegetable chart, page 94, but check the food before the specified time has elapsed. Steam heat is variable and foods may cook faster or slower than expected.

Wok steaming has an almost magical way of heightening food flavor. The delicate flavor of fish isn't lost in the cooking process. And steamed poultry can be an epicurean dish.

You will find wok steaming easy and the food so good. The wok has the unique ability to retain high heat, therefore foods cook quickly without excessive shrinkage. Instead of drying out, meats and poultry remain flavorful and juicy. Steamed foods also retain more nutrients than foods cooked by other cooking methods. Steaming is great for the calorie-counter, omitting the need for using oil.

POACHING

Foods can be poached in a wok as easily as stir-fried. Prepare food as directed in recipe. Place wok over medium-high heat. Add sufficient water or other liquid to come about 1/2 way up the side of the wok. Heat liquid until bubbles begin to break the surface. Do not allow liquid to boil vigorously. Spread paper towels or a cloth on a flat surface to arrange cooked food on for draining. Using a slotted spoon or flat skimmer, lower food gently into simmering liquid. Simmer as directed in recipe. Remove cooked food from wok with a spoon or skimmer. Drain slightly over wok; then place on prepared towels or cloth to drain well.

Steam small pieces of food in a dish over simmering water.

Steam large pieces of food directly on a rack or in a dish, if desired.

APPETIZERS

Today people are health conscious and care about how they look and feel. As a result, parties, buffets and other presentations of appetizers and beverages have changed. Lighter drinks are being served, such as wines, spritzers and many non-alcoholic beverages. Appetizers are being selected with a light touch in mind.

Recipes in this chapter are in tune with this trend. They are easy to prepare, have eye-appeal and are very delectable. Best of all, they are low in calories so all can enjoy them. Some appetizers are stir-fried, others are steamed or poached, but all have been prepared in a wok with a major thought in mind—keep the calories to a minimum.

Meatballs are always a treat as an appetizer. For your next party, serve Mini Chicken Balls with a choice of dipping sauces. Lean chicken breast minimizes calories, but doesn't cut down on flavor. Mini Turkey Balls are also a nice change from traditional beef meatballs.

For a kabob presentation, serve Pork & Pineapple Kabobs. What a great way to start out a Polynesian dinner party!

Vegetables make colorful appetizers. Pickled Mushrooms & Cocktail Onions are perfect for entertaining because they can be made ahead. At serving time, drain and spear each mushroom and onion on a wooden pick for an attractive presentation.

Menu

Breakfast
1/2 cantaloupe filled with 1/2 cup blueberries
1 bran muffin   1 teaspoon margarine
Coffee or tea
Lunch
Creole Red Beans & Rice, page 133
1 slice French bread
Dinner
Pickled Mushrooms & Cocktail Onions, page 27
Charleston Hangtown Stir-Fry, page 34
Espresso Custard with Lemon Topping, page 144
Coffee or tea
Snack
1/2 cup low-fat yogurt

About 1200 calories

Mini Chicken Balls

Serve at room temperature or hot from an electric wok, skillet or chafing dish, with dipping sauces.

Chicken Balls:

4 boneless chicken-breast halves, skinned
1 egg
2 teaspoons soy sauce

1 teaspoon fresh lemon juice
1 teaspoon onion juice
2 tablespoons cornstarch

Soy-Lemon Sauce:

1/4 cup fresh lemon juice

1/4 cup soy sauce

Hot-Hot Sauce:

2 teaspoons Dijon-style mustard
1/2 cup dry vermouth
1 cup Chicken Broth or Vegetable Broth,
   pages 152-153, canned broth or water

1/8 teaspoon dried leaf thyme
1/8 teaspoon dried leaf oregano
1 tablespoon tomato paste
1 teaspoon soy sauce

For chicken balls, cut chicken into small pieces. In a food processor fitted with a metal blade, process chicken until finely ground. Add egg, soy sauce, lemon juice, onion juice and cornstarch; process to a smooth paste. Or, grind chicken in a meat grinder; then place in a medium bowl. Stir in egg, soy sauce, lemon juice and onion juice. Sift cornstarch over mixture and your hands; knead to a smooth paste. Shape mixture into 36 (1-inch) balls. Fill wok about 1/2 full with water; bring to a simmer over medium heat. Using a slotted spoon, lower 8 balls into simmering water. Poach 6 to 8 minutes or until cooked through center. Remove with slotted spoon and drain well. Place on a plate. Repeat with remaining balls.

For soy-lemon sauce, in a small bowl, combine lemon juice and soy sauce.

For hot-hot sauce, in a 1-cup measure, stir together mustard and vermouth until smooth. Heat broth or water in a wok or medium saucepan over medium heat; stir in mustard mixture, thyme and oregano. Bring to a simmer. Stir in tomato paste and soy sauce until smooth.

To complete, serve meatballs hot or at room temperature with dipping sauces and cocktail picks for spearing. Makes 36 appetizers.

Variation

Prepare Hot-Hot Sauce; then place in an electric wok, skillet or chafing dish. Add chicken balls; stir to coat well. Keep warm until ready to serve.

About 14 calories per appetizer, 8 calories per tablespoon Soy-Lemon Sauce, and 12 calories per tablespoon Hot-Hot Sauce.

For onion juice, cut a large onion in 1/2. Grate over fine side of hand grater to obtain juice.

Mini Turkey Balls

A moist, delicious meatball that is low in calories.

3/4 cup soft bread crumbs
1/4 cup dry sherry or Madeira
1 lb. ground raw turkey
1 egg, lightly beaten
3 to 4 drops hot-pepper sauce
2 teaspoons soy sauce

1/4 teaspoon salt
1/8 teaspoon freshly ground black pepper
1/2 teaspoon ground oregano
2 cups Fresh Tomato Sauce or
    Quick Tomato Sauce, page 154

In a medium bowl, combine bread crumbs and sherry or Madeira; stir lightly. Cover and let stand 30 minutes or until liquid has been absorbed. In a food processor fitted with a metal blade, combine turkey, egg, bread-crumb mixture, hot-pepper sauce, soy sauce, salt, black pepper and oregano; process to a smooth paste. Or, combine all ingredients in a large bowl. Using your hands, blend thoroughly. Shape mixture into 24 (1-inch) balls. Fill wok about 1/2 full with water; bring to a simmer over medium heat. Add meatballs, about 1/3 at a time; poach 8 minutes or until cooked through center. Remove with a slotted spoon; drain well on paper towels. Repeat with remaining meatballs. Meatballs can be made to this point and refrigerated. To serve, reheat balls in tomato sauce in an electric wok, electric skillet or chafing dish. Serve hot with cocktail picks for spearing. Makes 24 appetizers.

About 40 calories per appetizer.

Potatoes with Chili-Cheese Dip

Plain potatoes can make elegant, great-tasting appetizers.

16 small new potatoes
4 oz. low-fat ricotta cheese
1/2 cup plain low-fat yogurt
1 tablespoon thawed frozen orange-juice
   concentrate

1/2 teaspoon pure chili powder
1/2 teaspoon ground cumin
Salt
Freshly ground black pepper
Garlic salt, if desired

Place unpeeled potatoes in a single layer on a rack in a wok over simmering water. Cover and steam 12 to 18 minutes or until tender. Remove from wok and let stand at room temperature; do not refrigerate. In a medium bowl, beat together cheese, yogurt and orange-juice concentrate until smooth. Stir in chili powder and cumin. Season to taste with salt, pepper and garlic salt, if desired. Cover and refrigerate until ready to serve. Serve potatoes with cocktail picks and chilled chili-cheese mixture as a dip. Makes 16 appetizers.

About 40 calories per appetizer.

Gold Coin Won Ton Appetizers

A favorite appetizer at the Gold Coin restaurant in New York and many tea houses in Chinatown.

1 tablespoon cornstarch
3 tablespoons water
2 teaspoons peanut oil or vegetable oil
1 boneless chicken-breast half,
 skinned, minced
1 teaspoon minced gingerroot
3/4 cup minced celery

1/4 cup finely chopped green onions
1/2 cup minced bamboo shoots
1/4 lb. mung bean sprouts, rinsed, drained,
 blotted dry, chopped
1 tablespoon hoisin sauce
1-1/2 teaspoons soy sauce
24 won ton wrappers

In a small bowl, stir together cornstarch and water until smooth; set aside. Place wok over high heat; add 1 teaspoon oil. When hot, add chicken; stir-fry 1 to 2 minutes or until meat is firm and white through center. Remove from wok with a slotted spoon; set aside. Add remaining 1 teaspoon oil to wok. When hot, add gingerroot, celery and green onions; stir-fry 1 minute or until vegetables are crisp-tender. Stir in bamboo shoots and bean sprouts. Stir cornstarch mixture, hoisin sauce, soy sauce and cooked chicken into wok. Stir until mixture thickens. Remove from wok; cool slightly. Remove won ton wrappers from package; cover with a slightly damp cloth to prevent them from drying out. Place a won ton wrapper with a corner facing you; spoon 1 teaspoon filling mixture onto center of side closest to you. Moisten edges of wrapper with water. Fold won ton in 1/2 to form a triangle; press edges together. Repeat with remaining won ton wrappers. Fill wok about 1/2 full with water. Bring to a simmer over medium heat. Add 1/3 of filled won tons; poach 4 to 5 minutes. Remove with slotted spoon; drain on paper towels. Repeat with remaining won tons. Serve hot or at room temperature with additional soy sauce for dipping. Makes 24 appetizers.

About 35 calories per appetizer.

Pork & Mushroom Won Tons

Won ton wrappers are found in the frozen food case or produce section of supermarkets.

1/2 cup mung bean sprouts
1/2 cup chopped mushrooms
4 green onions, chopped
1 cup chopped Chinese Red-Braised Pork,
 page 46

1 tablespoon Oriental chili sauce
 with garlic
1 teaspoon soy sauce
24 won ton wrappers

Place bean sprouts in a small bowl; cover with boiling water. Let stand 1 minute. Drain and blot dry with paper towels. In a chopping bowl or food processor fitted with a metal blade, combine bean sprouts, mushrooms, green onions and pork. Chop or process to a smooth paste. Add chili sauce and soy sauce; stir or process until blended. Follow directions above for filling and poaching won tons. Makes 24 appetizers.

About 35 calories per appetizer.

How to Make Gold Coin Won Tons

1/Place a won ton wrapper with corner facing you; spoon 1 teaspoon mixture onto center of side closest to you. Moisten wrapper edges with water.

2/Fold won ton in 1/2 to form a triangle; press edges together to seal. Repeat with remaining won ton wrappers and filling mixture.

Green-Beans Vinaigrette with Dip

Serve these flavorful beans with dip as an appetizer, or mix and serve as a first-course salad.

1 tablespoon peanut oil or vegetable oil	**1 lb. young green beans**
1 garlic clove, crushed	**1/4 cup sherry-wine vinegar**
1 (1-inch) piece gingerroot, crushed	**1/2 teaspoon salt**

Roquefort Dip:

4 oz. plain low-fat yogurt	**1/2 teaspoon salt**
4 oz. low-fat ricotta cheese	**1/4 teaspoon fresh ground black pepper**
2 or 3 dashes hot-pepper sauce	**2 oz. crumbled Roquefort or blue cheese**

For beans, place wok over high heat; add oil. When hot, add garlic and gingerroot; stir-fry until lightly browned. Remove and discard garlic and gingerroot. Add beans to wok; stir-fry 2 minutes. Add vinegar and salt; cover and steam 4 to 5 minutes or until beans are crisp-tender. Transfer beans and liquid to a medium bowl; cool slightly. Cover and refrigerate until chilled.

For dip, in a food processor fitted with a metal blade, place yogurt, ricotta cheese, hot-pepper sauce, salt and black pepper; process until smooth. Transfer to a medium bowl. Stir in Roquefort or blue cheese. Cover and refrigerate until chilled.

To serve, drain beans and serve as an appetizer with dip. Or, toss beans with 1/2 the dip. Then serve as a first-course salad. Reserve remaining dip for other use. Makes 8 appetizer servings or 4 salad servings.

About 90 calories per appetizer serving, 130 calories per salad serving.

Gold Coast Chicken Bites

Serve as an appetizer or as part of a buffet.

Mustard Dip:

1/4 cup dry white wine, beer or water

2 tablespoons dry mustard

Chicken Bites:

4 to 5 oz. fresh pearl onions
1 large garlic clove, minced
1 (1/2-inch) piece gingerroot, minced or
   1/2 teaspoon ground ginger
1/4 teaspoon turmeric
1/8 teaspoon red (cayenne) pepper or
   dried red-pepper flakes

About 3 tablespoons soy sauce
3 tablespoons dry sherry
1/2 cup Vegetable Broth, page 152, or water
1 teaspoon peanut oil or vegetable oil
1/4 lb. small mushrooms
1 lb. chicken thighs, skinned, boned,
   cut in bite-sized pieces
1 (8-oz.) can whole water chestnuts, drained

For mustard dip, in a small saucepan, heat wine, beer or water over medium heat; stir mustard into hot liquid. Remove from heat. Let stand 30 minutes to cool and for flavors to blend.

For chicken bites, in a small saucepan of water, boil unpeeled onions 3 minutes. Rinse in cold water, then drain. Cut off end of each onion; squeeze to slip off skin. In a small bowl, stir together garlic, ginger, turmeric, red pepper or red-pepper flakes, 3 tablespoons soy sauce, sherry, and broth or water. Place wok over high heat; add oil. When oil is hot, add mushrooms and peeled onions; stir-fry 1 minute. Sprinkle with 1 tablespoon soy-sauce mixture. Cover and cook about 1 minute or until mushrooms give off some liquid. Add chicken pieces, water chestnuts and remaining soy-sauce mixture; stir-fry about 1 minute. Cover and simmer 5 minutes. Remove cover and increase heat to high; stir-fry until liquid has evaporated. Serve hot with additional soy sauce and Mustard Dip. Makes 8 appetizer servings or 4 first-course servings.

About 105 calories per appetizer serving, 210 calories per first-course serving.

How to Make Chicken Pinwheels

1/Spread chicken pieces with spinach mixture. Roll up, jelly-roll style; secure with wooden picks.

2/Roll cooked chicken rolls in paprika. Cut each roll crosswise into slices.

Chicken Pinwheels

A steamed chicken appetizer that looks and tastes divine.

1 (10-oz.) pkg. thawed frozen
  chopped spinach
1 teaspoon peanut oil or vegetable oil
1 small onion, minced
1 teaspoon fresh lemon juice

2 oz. blue cheese, crumbled
Salt
Freshly ground black pepper
4 boneless chicken-breast halves, skinned
Paprika, if desired

Press out all liquid from spinach. Place wok over high heat; add oil. When hot, add onion; stir-fry about 30 seconds. Add drained spinach; stir-fry about 1 minute. Spoon mixture into a medium bowl; cool slightly. Stir in lemon juice and cheese. Season to taste with salt and pepper. Using the flat side of a cleaver or meat mallet, pound chicken pieces to about 1/4 inch thick. Spread each pounded chicken piece with spinach mixture. Roll up, jelly-roll style; secure with cocktail picks. Place filled chicken pieces in a single layer in a shallow steaming dish. Place dish on a rack in wok over simmering water; cover and steam 20 minutes or until meat is firm and white through center. Remove and cool slightly. Sprinkle with paprika, if desired. Cut each roll crosswise into 3 or 4 thin slices. Serve cut-side up. Makes 16 appetizers.

About 40 calories per appetizer.

Spicy Hot Shrimp

For those who like it hot and spicy.

2 teaspoons peanut oil or vegetable oil
3 tablespoons minced shallots
1-1/2 lbs. large shrimp, peeled, deveined
1 tablespoon Oriental chili sauce with
   garlic or 1 tablespoon spicy hot
   ketchup blended with 3 dashes hot-pepper
   sauce and a dash of garlic salt

About 3 tablespoons fresh lemon juice
Salt
Freshly ground black pepper

Place wok over high heat; add oil. When hot, add shallots; stir-fry 1 minute. Add shrimp; stir-fry 1 minute or until pink. Place shrimp in a medium bowl. Add chili sauce or ketchup, hot-pepper sauce and garlic salt; stir in lemon juice to taste. Season to taste with salt and black pepper. Cover and refrigerate 2 to 3 hours before serving. To serve, drain shrimp. Spear each with a cocktail pick. Makes about 24 appetizers.

About 30 calories per appetizer.

Shrimp in Pea Pods

A colorful, nutritious treat for your next cocktail party.

16 large shrimp, peeled, deveined,
   about 1 lb.

16 edible pea pods

Sherry-Vinaigrette Dressing:
1 tablespoon olive oil
1/4 cup Chicken Broth, page 153,
   canned broth or water
1 tablespoon sherry-wine vinegar

1 tablespoon fresh lemon juice
Salt
Freshly ground black pepper

In a wok over medium heat, bring 2 to 3 inches water to a simmer. Arrange shrimp in a single layer in a steaming dish. Place on a rack in wok over simmering water; cover and steam 3 minutes or until shrimp are pink.
For dressing, in a small deep bowl, stir together oil, broth or water, vinegar and lemon juice. Season with salt and pepper. Add hot shrimp to dressing; cover and marinate about 1 hour.
To complete, place pea pods in a large bowl; cover with boiling water. Let stand 1 minute; drain and rinse under cold running water to retain bright color. Split each pea pod along seam, leaving halves joined at 1 end. Remove shrimp, 1 at a time, from dressing, draining well. Place a shrimp in each split pea pod; secure each with a cocktail pick. Arrange on a platter. Cover and refrigerate until ready to serve. Makes 16 appetizers.

About 40 calories per appetizer.

Seafood-Pork Ball Appetizers

A light appetizer that's full of flavor.

12 oz. fish fillets
4 oz. bulk pork sausage
1/2 cup finely chopped green onions
1 teaspoon fresh lemon juice

1/2 teaspoon dry mustard
1/4 cup unsweetened apple juice
1/4 cup soy sauce

In a food processor fitted with a metal blade, combine fish, sausage, green onions, lemon juice and mustard; process to a moist paste. Or, place fish on a flat surface. With a cleaver or sharp knife, chop into very fine pieces. In a small bowl, combine chopped fish, sausage, green onions, lemon juice and mustard; blend to a moist paste. Shape mixture into 16 walnut-sized balls. Fill wok about 1/2 full with water. Place over high heat and bring to a simmer. Add balls, a few at a time. Cook, turning occasionally, about 10 minutes or until cooked through. Remove with a slotted spoon; drain well on paper towels. In a small bowl, combine apple juice and soy sauce; roll balls in mixture. Spear each appetizer with a cocktail pick. Serve hot or at room temperature. Makes 16 appetizers.

About 35 calories per appetizer.

Scallops with Teriyaki Sauce

A delicious dish, great for parties.

1 teaspoon sugar
2 teaspoons saké or dry white wine
1 tablespoon mirin or cream sherry
2 tablespoons soy sauce
1/4 cup all-purpose flour

1/2 teaspoon white pepper
1 lb. sea scallops
1 tablespoon peanut oil or vegetable oil
2 or 3 crisp lettuce leaves

In a 2-cup measure, stir together sugar, saké or white wine, mirin or sherry, and soy sauce until sugar is dissolved; set aside. In a pie plate or small plastic bag, combine flour and white pepper. Coat each scallop with flour mixture; shake off excess flour leaving a thin coating. Place wok over high heat; add oil. When hot, add enough scallops to cover bottom of wok. Cook 1-1/2 minutes; turn and cook other side. Remove from wok with a slotted spoon. Cook remaining scallops in batches as necessary. When all scallops are cooked, pour off any remaining oil; return wok to medium heat. Add sugar mixture to wok; cook, stirring constantly, until mixture slightly thickens. Add cooked scallops; cook, turning in simmering liquid until well coated, about 1 minute. Remove from wok with slotted spoon. Arrange lettuce on a serving plate; top with cooked scallops. Serve with remaining sauce as a dip. Makes 8 appetizer servings.

About 80 calories per serving.

Pork & Pineapple Kabobs

An attractive appetizer to serve on cocktail picks or small skewers.

1/2 lb. lean boneless pork,
   cut in 24 (1/2-inch) cubes
1/4 cup fresh lemon juice
4 or 5 thin strips lemon peel
1 small garlic clove, minced
1 teaspoon dried leaf thyme
1 teaspoon dried leaf basil
1 bay leaf, crumbled
5 teaspoons peanut oil or
   vegetable oil

2 tablespoons red-wine vinegar
1 (8-oz.) can pineapple chunks in
   unsweetened juice
1/2 cup Chicken Broth, page 153,
   canned broth or water
2 tablespoons apple brandy or apple jack
2 teaspoons cornstarch
12 pickled cocktail onions

In a large bowl, combine pork, lemon juice, lemon peel, garlic, thyme, basil and bay leaf. Stir in 3 teaspoons oil and vinegar. Cover and refrigerate up to 24 hours. Remove pork from marinade; blot dry with paper towels. Place wok over medium-high heat; add remaining 2 teaspoons oil. When hot, add pork; stir-fry 3 minutes or until pork is no longer pink. Drain pineapple juice into wok; reserve pineapple. Reduce heat and simmer until juice evaporates. Remove from heat. In a small saucepan, stir together broth or water, brandy and cornstarch until smooth. Cook over medium heat, stirring until sauce is clear and thickened; remove from heat. Cover and keep warm. Using 12 cocktail picks or small skewers, thread 2 cooked pork cubes, 1 cocktail onion and 1 pineapple chunk on each pick or skewer. Place kabobs in a chafing dish; pour sauce over kabobs. Keep warm until ready to serve. Makes 12 appetizers.

About 70 calories per appetizer.

Vegetable Platter with Tapenade Dip, page 24.

Vegetable Platter with Tapenade Dip

Photo on page 23.

Too beautiful, too flavorful to resist.

16 fresh pearl onions
2 tablespoons olive oil
1/4 cup fresh lemon juice
1 small garlic clove, minced
1/2 teaspoon salt
1 cup cauliflowerets
2 small yellow summer squash,
   cut on an angle in 1/2-inch-thick slices

Tapenade Dip:
1/4 cup pitted Greek olives
1 (2-oz.) can caper-stuffed anchovy
   fillets in olive oil
2 tablespoons flaked tuna
1 tablespoon fresh lemon juice

1 zucchini, cut in 1/4-inch slices
1 small green bell pepper,
   cut in 1/2-inch strips
1 small red bell pepper,
   cut in 1/2-inch strips
16 cherry tomatoes
Green-onion brushes, opposite
Chrysanthemum radishes, opposite

1/2 cup fresh chopped basil, or
   1/4 cup minced parsley and
   2 teaspoons dried leaf basil
1 cup plain low-fat yogurt

For vegetables, in a small saucepan of water, boil unpeeled onions 3 minutes. Rinse in cold water and drain. Cut off end of each onion; squeeze to slip off skin. Pour olive oil and lemon juice into a shallow steaming dish; add garlic and salt. Place dish on a rack in a wok over simmering water. Cut a small **X** in root end of each onion. Add peeled onions to olive-oil mixture in steaming dish; stir lightly to coat. Cover and steam 10 to 15 minutes or until onions are easily pierced. Remove onions with a large slotted spoon, draining any liquid back into steaming dish. Add cauliflowerets; stir gently to coat with liquid. Cover and steam 2 minutes. Add summer squash and zucchini; cover and steam 3 minutes or until crisp-tender. Remove with slotted spoon. Add bell peppers; cover and steam 2 minutes. Remove steamer dish from wok. Place each vegetable in a separate storage container; drizzle with remaining steaming liquid. Cover and refrigerate until chilled.
For dip, in a food processor fitted with a metal blade, combine olives, anchovy fillets with oil, tuna, lemon juice and basil or minced parsley and dried basil. Cover and process until finely chopped. Add yogurt; process until smooth. Transfer to a small bowl; cover and refrigerate until chilled or ready to serve.
To serve, place dip in center of a large platter. Drain each vegetable; arrange separately in pie-shaped wedges. Garnish with green-onion brushes and chrysanthemum radishes. Serve with cocktail picks for spearing. Makes 12 appetizer servings.

About 70 calories per serving.

How to Make Vegetable Garnishes

1/Green-Onion Brushes—Trim root off onion; cut off tip, leaving 3 inches of stalk. Make four crisscross cuts, 1-inch deep, into both ends of stalk. Place in iced water until onions fan open.

2/Chrysanthemum Radishes—Peel top half of radish; then make fine checkerboard cuts through top, leaving bottom intact. Place in iced water until ready to use.

Poorman's Caviar

A wonderful flavor, great to serve with crisp crackers as a first course.

1 small eggplant, about 1 lb.
About 2 tablespoons salt
2 teaspoons peanut oil or vegetable oil
2 tablespoons water
1 tablespoon red-wine vinegar
1 small onion, minced
1 small garlic clove, minced
1 (16-oz.) can peeled tomatoes

2 tablespoons chopped fresh basil or
  2 teaspoons dried leaf basil
1/2 teaspoon dry mustard
2 to 3 dashes hot-pepper sauce
Salt
Freshly ground black pepper
Paprika
Crisp crackers or lettuce leaves

Peel eggplant; cut into small cubes. Place eggplant in layers in a large colander, sprinkling each layer lightly with salt. Let stand 30 minutes. Rinse eggplant under cold running water; pat dry with paper towels. Place wok over medium heat; add oil. When hot, add eggplant cubes; stir-fry about 1 minute. Sprinkle with water and vinegar; cover and steam 1 minute. Add onion; stir-fry 1 minute or until soft. Stir in garlic, tomatoes with juice, basil, mustard and hot-pepper sauce. Stir to break up tomatoes. Cover and steam, stirring occasionally, 3 to 4 minutes or until eggplant is tender. Place in a blender or food processor fitted with a metal blade; process until smooth. Season to taste with salt and black pepper. Spoon into a serving dish. Cover and refrigerate until chilled. To serve, sprinkle with paprika. As an appetizer, serve with crisp crackers. As a first course, spoon onto lettuce-lined plates. Makes 10 appetizer servings or 6 first-course servings.

About 30 calories per appetizer serving, 50 calories per first-course serving.

Tabbouleh-Stuffed Mushrooms

A flavorful Middle Eastern salad mix makes these stuffed mushrooms deliciously different.

1/2 cup bulgur
1 large tomato
12 large mushrooms
3 teaspoons peanut oil or vegetable oil
1 large onion, minced
1 small garlic clove, minced
1/2 cup finely chopped fresh
   Italian parsley

1/2 cup fresh lemon juice
1 tablespoon olive oil
1/2 teaspoon salt
1/8 teaspoon freshly ground black pepper
1 tablespoon finely chopped fresh
   mint leaves or 1 teaspoon dried leaf mint

Place bulgur in a medium bowl; add boiling water to cover by 1 inch. Cover and let stand 1 hour or until water has been absorbed. Place bulgur on a clean towel; roll up and squeeze thoroughly to remove excess water. Transfer to a large bowl; fluff with a fork. Cut tomato in 1/2; squeeze out and discard seeds and juice. Finely chop tomato halves; blot dry with paper towel. Trim mushroom stems. Holding each mushroom under cold running water, rub clean; blot dry with paper towel. Remove mushroom stems, reserving caps; finely chop stems. Place wok over medium-high heat; add 2 teaspoons peanut oil or vegetable oil. When hot, add chopped mushroom stems, onion and garlic; stir-fry until crisp-tender. Stir mixture into soaked bulgur. Add chopped tomato, parsley, 1/3 cup lemon juice, olive oil, salt, pepper and mint. Cover and refrigerate until ready to use. To serve, place wok over medium heat; add remaining 1 teaspoon oil. When hot, add mushroom caps; stir-fry 1 minute or until caps begin to darken. Place in a medium bowl; toss with remaining lemon juice. Fill each mushroom cap with bulgur mixture. Makes 12 appetizers.

About 60 calories per appetizer.

Bulgur is wheat kernels that have been cooked, dried and cracked. Look for it in the grain section of your supermarket or in health-food stores.

Pickled Mushrooms & Cocktail Onions

No one will deny that these pickled mushrooms are delicious.

1 cup tarragon vinegar or
  other mild vinegar
1 tablespoon olive oil
2 tablespoons water
8 whole cloves
1 bay leaf
1 teaspoon salt

1 teaspoon sugar
2 or 3 dashes hot-pepper sauce
1 tablespoon peanut oil or vegetable oil
1 garlic clove, crushed
1 (1-inch) piece gingerroot, crushed
36 button mushrooms, about 1/2 lb.
36 pickled cocktail onions

In a medium saucepan, combine vinegar, olive oil, water, cloves, bay leaf, salt, sugar and hot-pepper sauce. Place over medium heat; bring to a boil. Remove from heat, but keep warm. Place wok over high heat; add peanut oil or vegetable oil. When hot, add garlic and gingerroot; stir-fry until lightly browned. Remove and discard garlic and gingerroot. Add mushrooms to wok; stir-fry 1 minute. Cover and steam 30 seconds. Transfer mushrooms and cooking liquid to a large bowl. Add vinegar mixture to bowl; cover and refrigerate until chilled. To serve, drain mushrooms, discarding marinade. Spear 1 cocktail onion and 1 mushroom onto each of 36 cocktail picks. Makes 36 appetizers.

About 11 calories per appetizer.

HOW TO PURCHASE AND STORE MUSHROOMS

Choose mushrooms with caps completely closed over the stem showing no gills. Open caps indicate older mushrooms. Mushrooms should be firm, even-shaped and unbruised. Avoid wilted, slick or wrinkled mushrooms. The Champignon de Paris variety is the most commercially grown mushroom available in the United States. These mushrooms range in color from white or creamy-white to tan. Their size ranges from 3/4 inch to 3 inches in diameter. Store them in a paper bag in the refrigerator. Trim stems and wipe off caps with a damp cloth just before using.

MEAT

Overall meat consumption today is down as people are more conscious of their dietary needs. By cooking meat in a wok, you can reduce calories without sacrificing flavor. Keeping with our calorie-cutting program, meat servings have been established at 3 to 4 ounces. Meats are usually cooked in a dry wok. They are thinly sliced and stir-fried with vegetables, steamed, or ground and blended with other low-calorie foods. You can enjoy these dishes without any guilt.

It is important to select tender beef cuts for quick wok cooking. Ideal beef cuts include sirloin, tenderloin, top round and lean ground beef. Less-tender cuts, such as flank, can be used; however, they should be marinated to aid in tenderizing and then cooked just until they lose their pink color.

For money savings, large cuts of meat can be purchased and then cut at home or by your butcher to your specifications. Most butchers will even cut sale-priced meats to order. This is an excellent way to cut cost as well as calories. Be sure to package meats in heavy-duty foil, freezer bags or airtight containers for proper storage. Label packages with weight, date and name of meat cut before storing.

To prepare meats for cutting in small strips, place meat in the freezer until very firm. Then cut meat across the grain into thin slices; cut slices in 1/4-inch-wide strips. Stir-fry meat strips alone or in combination with vegetables, pasta or rice for a wide range of taste-tempting dishes.

Menu

Breakfast
1/2 grapefruit
1 poached egg on thin-sliced whole-wheat toast
Coffee or tea

Snack
1/2 cup low-fat yogurt

Lunch
1 cup Vegetable Broth, page 152
4 to 6 Tofu Croutons, page 151
1 Golden Apple, page 138

Dinner
3 Gold Coin Won Tons, page 16
Pork & Scallop Stir-Fry, page 77
Lemony Low-Calorie Sponge Cake, page 147
Coffee or tea

About 1200 calories

Quick & Easy Beef Stew

The hearty taste of old-fashioned stew without extra calories or hours in the kitchen.

1 tablespoon dry sherry
1 small garlic clove, crushed
2 teaspoons soy sauce
3 teaspoons peanut oil or vegetable oil
3/4 lb. beef top round, cut in thin strips
4 small new potatoes
2 carrots, cut in 1/2-inch chunks
1/2 lb. young green beans

1 teaspoon cornstarch
1-1/2 cups Beef Broth or Vegetable Broth,
  page 152, canned broth or water
1 tablespoon thick steak sauce
1 onion, coarsely chopped
1/4 lb. mushrooms, coarsely
  chopped if large, whole if small

In a shallow dish, stir together sherry, garlic, soy sauce and 1 teaspoon oil. Add beef strips; stir to coat. Cover and refrigerate 30 minutes. Place potatoes and carrots in a steamer dish on a rack in a wok over simmering water; cover and steam 10 minutes or until tender. Remove from wok; set aside. If necessary, add additional water to wok to come just below steamer rack. Place green beans in steamer dish on rack in wok over simmering water; cover and steam 6 to 8 minutes or until crisp-tender. Remove from wok; set aside with carrots and potatoes. Remove rack from wok; pour off and discard water. Wipe dry with paper towels. In a small bowl, stir together cornstarch, broth or water, and steak sauce until smooth; set aside. Place wok over high heat; add remaining 2 teaspoons oil. Drain beef strips. When oil is hot, add drained beef strips; stir-fry until lightly browned. Add onion and mushrooms; stir-fry 1 minute. Add steamed potatoes, carrots and beans; stir-fry 1 minute. Cover and steam 30 seconds. Stir-fry until vegetables are heated through. Stir cornstarch mixture into wok, blending with vegetables. Cook, stirring frequently, until sauce is slightly thickened. Serve immediately. Makes 4 servings.

About 220 calories per serving.

Restaurant-Style Sukiyaki

Tender, juicy, steam-stirred beef makes this an outstanding sukiyaki.

1 lb. beef tenderloin, cut in thin strips
1-1/2 cups Japanese-Style Stock, page 151;
   Chicken Broth, page 153;
   canned broth or water
2 tablespoons rice wine or dry sherry
About 1 teaspoon sugar
1/4 lb. firm tofu, rinsed,
   drained, blotted dry

1 large onion, chopped
1 garlic clove, minced
6 to 8 green onions, cut in 1-inch pieces
1 sweet potato, cut in thin slices
1 turnip, cut in thin slices
2 cups shredded bok choy or Chinese cabbage
Soy sauce

Using the flat side of a cleaver or meat mallet, lightly pound beef strips. In a small bowl, stir together broth or water, wine or sherry, and 1 teaspoon sugar. Cut tofu in 1/4-inch cubes. Place wok over medium heat; add broth mixture. Bring to a simmer; add onion, garlic, green onions, sweet potato and turnip. Cover and simmer 4 to 5 minutes or until vegetables are crisp-tender. Stir in tofu cubes and bok choy or Chinese cabbage. Place beef strips over vegetables; sprinkle lightly with sugar. Cover and steam 1 minute or until beef is lightly browned. Toss beef and vegetables together. Season to taste with soy sauce. Makes 4 servings.

About 240 calories per serving.

Stir-Fried Beef with Vegetables Americana

An American favorite, slimmed down.

2-1/4 teaspoons peanut oil or
   vegetable oil
1 (8-oz.) pkg. vermicelli
1 tablespoon thick steak sauce
3/4 cup Vegetable Broth or Beef Broth,
   page 152, canned broth or water
1/2 lb. beef sirloin, cut in thin strips

2 large onions, cut in thin wedges
2 small green bell peppers,
   cut in thin strips
2 celery stalks, thinly sliced
6 large mushrooms, coarsely chopped
Salt
Freshly ground black pepper

In a large saucepan, bring 3 to 4 quarts water to a boil. Add 1/4 teaspoon oil and vermicelli; cook according to package directions until tender but firm to the bite. While pasta cooks, in a small bowl, stir together steak sauce and broth or water. Place wok over high heat; add remaining 2 teaspoons oil. When hot, add beef strips; stir-fry until lightly browned. Remove with a slotted spoon; set aside. Add onions, bell peppers, celery and mushrooms to wok; stir-fry until crisp-tender. Add steak-sauce mixture and browned beef strips to wok; cook, stirring constantly, until slightly thickened. Season to taste with salt and black pepper. Drain cooked pasta. Serve beef mixture over hot cooked vermicelli. Makes 4 servings.

About 340 calories per serving.

Steak & Pepper Stir-Fry

A classic stir-fry with great taste.

1 tablespoon thick steak sauce
1 teaspoon Dijon-style mustard
1 teaspoon cornstarch
1 cup Vegetable Broth or Beef Broth,
   page 152, canned broth or water
1/2 lb. beef sirloin, cut in thin strips

1 teaspoon freshly ground black pepper
2 teaspoons peanut oil or vegetable oil
1 small onion, chopped
1 small green bell pepper,
   cut in thin strips
1 cup hot cooked rice

In a small bowl, stir together steak sauce, mustard, cornstarch and broth or water until smooth; set aside. Sprinkle beef strips with black pepper; using the flat side of a cleaver or meat mallet, pound pepper into strips. Place wok over medium heat; add oil. When hot, add seasoned beef strips; stir-fry until lightly browned. Stir in onion and bell pepper; stir-fry 30 seconds. Add steak-sauce mixture to wok; bring to a boil, stirring constantly, until slightly thickened. Serve over hot cooked rice. Makes 2 servings.

About 300 calories per serving.

Beef with Red, White & Green Vegetables

Steam the beef over the vegetables, then stir together for a colorful blend.

1/2 lb. beef flank steak
2 tablespoons soy sauce
1 teaspoon sesame oil
1 tablespoon dry sherry
1 large tomato
1/2 cup plus 3 tablespoons Beef Broth or
   Vegetable Broth, page 152,
   canned broth or water

2 teaspoons cornstarch
2 teaspoons peanut oil or vegetable oil
1 small garlic clove, crushed
1 (1-inch) piece gingerroot, crushed
2 cups broccoli flowerets
2 cups shredded romaine
2 cups hot cooked rice

Using the flat side of a cleaver or meat mallet, pound steak to tenderize; then cut crosswise into 1/8-inch-thick strips. Place strips in a shallow dish; sprinkle with 1 tablespoon soy sauce, sesame oil and sherry. Cover and refrigerate 30 minutes. Cut tomato in 1/2; squeeze out and discard seeds and juice. Cut tomato halves into narrow strips; blot dry with paper towels. In a small bowl, stir together 1/2 cup broth or water, cornstarch and remaining 1 tablespoon soy sauce until smooth; set aside. Place wok over high heat; add oil. When hot, add garlic and gingerroot; stir-fry until lightly browned. Remove and discard garlic and gingerroot. Add broccoli and tomato strips to wok; stir-fry 1 minute. Stir in remaining 3 tablespoons broth or water. Cover and steam 1 to 2 minutes. Arrange beef strips on top of vegetables; pour any remaining marinade mixture over top. Cover and steam 2 minutes. Stir beef down into vegetables. Stir cornstarch mixture into vegetable mixture until slightly thickened. Stir-fry 30 seconds. Stir in romaine; cover and steam 30 seconds. Serve over hot cooked rice. Makes 4 servings.

About 270 calories per serving.

Beef & Broccoli Stir-Fry

The spicy, tart marinade helps tenderize the beef round steak.

2 tablespoons soy sauce
2 tablespoons red-wine vinegar
1 teaspoon Oriental chili sauce with garlic
   or 1 crushed garlic clove and
   1 teaspoon pure chili powder
2 tablespoons water
3/4 lb. beef top round,
   cut in 1/4-inch-thick strips

1 bunch broccoli, about 1 lb.
2 teaspoons peanut oil or vegetable oil
1 medium onion, chopped
1 cup Quick Tomato Sauce, page 154
1 cup shredded bok choy or romaine
1 carrot, cut lengthwise in
   1/4-inch-thick strips
1 cup cold cooked rice

In a heavy plastic bag, combine soy sauce, vinegar, chili sauce or garlic and chili powder, and water. Add beef strips; close bag securely. Shake bag to coat beef strips evenly. Place bag in a large bowl; refrigerate up to 18 hours, turning bag occasionally. Break broccoli flowerets from stems; trim stems, then cut lengthwise in 1/4-inch-thick strips. Place broccoli flowerets in a pan of lightly salted cold water. Let stand 15 minutes. Drain broccoli; pat dry with paper towels. Drain beef, reserving marinade; blot dry with paper towels. Place wok over high heat; add 1 teaspoon oil. When hot, add beef strips; stir-fry 1 minute. Remove beef strips; add remaining 1 teaspoon oil. When hot, add onion and broccoli stems; stir-fry 1 minute. Add broccoli flowerets, browned beef strips, reserved marinade and tomato sauce; bring to a boil. Stir in bok choy or romaine, carrot and rice. Cook until mixture is bubbly and hot. Makes 4 servings.

About 255 calories per serving.

Chinese-American Beef

A flavor you are sure to enjoy.

1/4 teaspoon peanut oil or vegetable oil
1 onion, chopped
1 small green bell pepper, chopped
1 garlic clove, minced
2 tablespoons Madeira
1 tablespoon soy sauce

3/4 lb. lean ground beef
1 cup fresh or thawed frozen green peas
1 cup cold cooked rice
1/2 cup thinly sliced water chestnuts
2 tablespoons thinly sliced green onion

Place wok over high heat; add 1/4 teaspoon oil. When hot, add onion and bell pepper; stir-fry about 1 minute. Add garlic; stir-fry about 30 seconds. Add Madeira, soy sauce and ground beef. Stir-fry, breaking up beef, until beef is lightly browned. Stir in peas; stir-fry until peas are nearly cooked. Stir in rice and water chestnuts. Cook, stirring constantly, until hot. Serve garnished with green onion. Makes 4 servings.

About 160 calories per serving.

How to Make Rinderrouladen

1/Sprinkle meat slices with pepper and mustard. Place green beans, onion strips and pickle strips on narrow end of slices.

2/Roll and secure with wooden picks. Place wok over high heat. When hot, add beef rolls; brown on all sides.

Rinderrouladen

Stuffed beef rolls are a popular German specialty.

1 (2-inch-thick) beef top round, cut in 8 (1/4-inch-thick) slices
2 tablespoons soy sauce
2 tablespoons fresh lemon juice
1 lb. young green beans
6 green onions

2 small dill pickles
1/4 teaspoon freshly ground black pepper
1 teaspoon dry mustard
2 teaspoons peanut oil or vegetable oil
1/2 cup Beef Broth, page 152, canned broth or water

Using the flat side of a cleaver or meat mallet, pound beef slices to flatten. Place pounded slices in a long, shallow dish. Sprinkle with soy sauce and lemon juice, turning to coat evenly. Cover and refrigerate several hours or until ready to use. Place green beans on a rack in a wok over simmering water. Cover and steam 6 to 8 minutes or until crisp-tender; cool to room temperature. Trim green onions, cutting off all but about 1 inch of tops; reserve tops. Cut onion tops into thin rounds. Cut bottom parts of onions lengthwise into slivers. Trim ends from each dill pickle; cut each lengthwise into 8 strips. Drain meat, reserving marinade. Blot each strip with paper towels, then place on a flat work surface. Sprinkle meat slices with pepper and mustard. Place 4 or 5 green beans, 2 or 3 onion strips and 2 dill-pickle strips on narrow end of slice; roll and secure with wooden picks. Place wok over high heat; add oil. When hot, add beef rolls; brown on all sides, turning rolls gently with a spatula. Add broth or water; cover and steam 4 to 5 minutes. Uncover and cook beef rolls, turning frequently, until liquid has evaporated. To serve, transfer to a platter; sprinkle with reserved marinade and green-onion tops. Makes 8 beef rolls or 4 servings.

About 210 calories per serving.

Charleston Hangtown Stir-Fry

Steak, oysters and mushrooms — a fantastic flavor combination.

2 tablespoons soy sauce
1 teaspoon Oriental chili sauce with garlic
   or 1 garlic clove, crushed and
   1/2 teaspoon pure chili powder
1 teaspoon Oriental fish sauce, if desired
3/4 lb. beef flank steak
1 (10-oz.) pkg. frozen Japanese-style
   vegetables in light sauce
1 tablespoon dry sherry

1 cup water
2 teaspoons cornstarch
1 cup large shucked oysters
2 teaspoons peanut oil or vegetable oil
4 large mushrooms, coarsely chopped
1 cup hot cooked rice
1 cup mung bean sprouts, rinsed,
   drained, blotted dry

In a shallow baking dish, stir together 1 tablespoon soy sauce, chili sauce or garlic and chili powder, and fish sauce, if desired. Using the flat side of a cleaver or meat mallet, pound steak to tenderize; then cut crosswise into thin strips. Add beef strips to soy-sauce mixture; stir to coat. Cover and refrigerate 1 to 3 hours. Cook frozen vegetables according to package directions, reducing cooking time 2 to 3 minutes; set aside. In a small bowl, stir together remaining 1 tablespoon soy sauce, sherry, water and cornstarch until smooth. Drain oysters; place on paper towels to dry. Drain beef strips, reserving marinade; blot dry with paper towels. Place wok over high heat; add 1 teaspoon oil. When hot, add mushrooms; stir-fry about 1 minute. Remove from wok. Add remaining 1 teaspoon oil to wok. When hot, add beef strips; stir-fry until lightly browned. Add cooked vegetables; stir-fry 30 seconds. Stir in cooked mushrooms, drained oysters and reserved marinade from beef; stir-fry until edges of oysters begin to curl. Add cornstarch mixture to wok; cook, stirring constantly, until slightly thickened. Serve over hot cooked rice and bean sprouts. Makes 4 servings.

About 290 calories per serving.

TO CLEAN MUNG BEANS OR OTHER SPROUTS

Place sprouts in a large bowl of cold water. Skim off loose hulls and root ends which float to the top. Pour off top water along with any foreign matter; lift sprouts, leaving sand and dirt in bottom of bowl. Blot sprouts dry with paper towels.

Steak with Deviled Sauce

Delicious served with steamed new potatoes and green beans.

1 lb. beef flank steak
Salt
Freshly ground black pepper
1 teaspoon peanut oil or vegetable oil
2 tablespoons finely chopped shallots
1/2 cup Vegetable Broth or Chicken Broth,
  pages 152-153, canned broth or water

2 tablespoons cognac or other brandy
1 teaspoon Dijon-style mustard
1 tablespoon thick steak sauce
1 tablespoon minced fresh parsley
2 cups shredded iceberg lettuce

Using the flat side of a cleaver or meat mallet, pound steak to tenderize; then cut crosswise into thin strips. Season beef strips with salt and pepper; pound seasoning into strips. Place wok over high heat. When hot, add steak strips, a few at a time; cook 2 minutes on each side until lightly browned. Remove strips as cooked; keep warm. Remove wok from heat; wipe clean with paper towels. Place wok over medium heat; add oil. When hot, add shallots; stir-fry 1 minute. Add broth or water, brandy, mustard and steak sauce; bring to a boil, cooking until reduced by 1/2. Stir in parsley and steak strips; stir-fry until hot. Serve over lettuce. Makes 4 servings.

About 180 calories per serving.

Carne Asada

For a south-of-the-border treat, serve this great-tasting, Mexican-style steak.

1 lb. thick-sliced beef top round, cut in
  1/8-inch-thick slices
About 4 teaspoons pure chili powder
2 tablespoons red-wine vinegar
4 teaspoons peanut oil or vegetable oil
1/2 teaspoon sugar
1 small garlic clove, minced

Salt
Freshly ground black pepper
1/2 cup Beef Broth, page 152,
  canned broth or water
1 small Vidalia onion or other sweet onion,
  thinly sliced

Using the flat side of a cleaver or meat mallet, pound meat to tenderize. Sprinkle slices with chili powder to taste. In a small bowl, combine vinegar, 3 teaspoons oil, sugar and garlic. Place beef slices in a heavy plastic bag; add vinegar mixture. Close bag; refrigerate 8 to 24 hours. Remove beef from marinade; scrape off garlic pieces. Blot beef dry with paper towels. Sprinkle beef slices with salt and pepper; press seasoning into meat. Let stand 20 minutes. Place wok over high heat; add remaining 1 teaspoon oil. When hot, add beef; stir-fry 1-1/2 minutes or until lightly browned. Transfer to a serving dish. Pour broth or water into wok; add onion. Stir-fry until onion is hot and liquid is reduced to 2 tablespoons. Remove from heat; top meat with onion. Drizzle cooking liquid over meat. Makes 4 servings.

About 180 calories per serving.

Greek-Style Pitaburgers

Tahini dip and dressing mix can be found in the gourmet section of most supermarkets.

1/4 cup water
1 teaspoon tahini dip and dressing mix
1 teaspoon cornstarch
4 oz. firm tofu, rinsed, drained,
    blotted dry
1/2 lb. lean ground beef
1 teaspoon soy sauce

2 teaspoons peanut oil or vegetable oil
1 garlic clove, crushed
1 cup mung bean sprouts, rinsed, drained,
    blotted dry
1 tablespoon Italian-style capers,
    drained, chopped
4 (4-inch-round) pita breads, split open

In a small bowl, stir together water, tahini mix and cornstarch until smooth. In a large bowl, flake tofu with a fork. Add beef and soy sauce; blend thoroughly. Place wok over high heat; add oil. When hot, add garlic; stir-fry until lightly browned. Remove and discard garlic. Add tofu mixture to wok; stir-fry until beef is lightly browned. Stir cornstarch mixture into beef mixture; stir-fry until slightly thickened. Stir in bean sprouts and capers until heated through. Spoon hot beef mixture into pita breads. Garnish with chopped green onion and tomatoes, if desired. Makes 4 servings.

About 230 calories per serving.

Beef & Oriental Vegetable Stir-Fry

A gourmet feast in a wok.

1 small tomato
3/4 lb. lean ground beef
1 tablespoon Madeira
1 teaspoon peanut oil or vegetable oil
1 small Vidalia onion or
    other sweet onion, chopped
1/4 lb. large mushrooms, quartered
2 tablespoons Beef Broth, page 152,
    canned broth or water

2 cups finely shredded bok choy
1/2 cup mung bean sprouts, rinsed,
    drained, blotted dry
4 water chestnuts, thinly sliced
1 cup hot cooked rice
1 tablespoon thinly sliced green onion

Cut tomato in 1/2; squeeze out and discard seeds and juice. Cut tomato halves into narrow strips; blot strips dry with paper towels. In a medium bowl, combine ground beef and Madeira. Place wok over high heat; add oil. When hot, add onion and mushrooms; stir-fry 1 minute. Stir in beef mixture; stir-fry until lightly browned. Sprinkle beef with broth or water; cover and steam 1 minute. Add bok choy and bean sprouts; stir-fry 1 minute. Add water chestnuts, tomato strips and rice; stir-fry until heated through. Serve garnished with green onion. Makes 4 servings.

About 240 calories per serving.

Greek-Style Pitaburgers

Near-Eastern Stir-Fry

Tofu adds protein without adding a lot of extra calories.

1 (10-oz.) pkg. frozen mixed
   Japanese-style vegetables
3/4 cup Beef Broth, page 152,
   canned broth or water
1 teaspoon cornstarch
2 tablespoons soy sauce
1 tablespoon tahini dip and dressing mix,
   if desired
6 oz. firm tofu, rinsed, drained,
   blotted dry

1/2 lb. lean ground beef
2 teaspoons peanut oil or vegetable oil
1 small onion, chopped
4 large mushrooms, quartered
4 small radishes, thinly sliced
2 cups shredded bok choy, Chinese cabbage
   or green cabbage
4 Greek olives, chopped
2 cups hot cooked rice
1 tablespoon minced green onion

In a saucepan of boiling water, cook frozen vegetables 2 to 3 minutes or until vegetables can be separated; set aside. In a small bowl, stir together broth or water, cornstarch, 1 tablespoon soy sauce and tahini mix, if desired, until smooth; set aside. In a large bowl, flake tofu with a fork. Add ground beef and remaining 1 tablespoon soy sauce; blend thoroughly. Shape mixture into 1 large patty. Place wok over medium-high heat; add oil. When hot, add patty; cook 1 to 1-1/2 minutes or until lightly browned on each side. Add cornstarch mixture; cover and steam 2 to 3 minutes. Uncover and cook until broth is reduced to about 2 tablespoons and bottom of patty is browned. Turn and brown other side. Break patty into chunks. Add onion, mushrooms and radishes; stir-fry 30 seconds. Stir in Japanese-style vegetables; stir-fry 1 minute. Add bok choy or cabbage and olives. Stir until hot and sauce has slightly thickened. Serve over hot cooked rice. Garnish with green onion. Makes 4 servings.

About 320 calories per serving.

Beef with Peas & Rice

A favorite to prepare ahead; reheat when ready to serve.

1 tablespoon soy sauce
1 tablespoon dry sherry
1 teaspoon sugar
1/4 cup water
2 teaspoons cornstarch
2 teaspoons peanut oil or vegetable oil

3/4 lb. lean ground beef
1/4 cup minced celery
1/4 cup finely chopped green onions
1 (10-oz.) pkg. thawed frozen green peas
   or 10 oz. fresh shelled peas, blanched
1 cup hot cooked rice

In a small bowl, stir together soy sauce, sherry, sugar, water and cornstarch until smooth; set aside. Place wok over high heat; add oil. When hot, add ground beef; stir-fry, breaking up meat, until lightly browned. Stir in celery and green onions; stir-fry 1 minute. Stir in peas and cornstarch mixture; cover and steam 30 seconds. Uncover and stir-fry 1 minute or until peas are tender and liquid is thickened. Stir in rice. Serve immediately or reheat to serve. Makes 4 servings.

About 280 calories per serving.

Korean Beef with Vegetables

Use leftover cooked roast beef to make this dish extra quick.

1/2 lb. medium-rare or rare cooked beef,
   thinly sliced
1 garlic clove, crushed
1 (1-inch) piece gingerroot, crushed
1 teaspoon sesame oil
2 tablespoons soy sauce
1 teaspoon sugar
1/4 teaspoon dried red-pepper flakes
1/4 teaspoon Chinese Five-Spice Powder,
   page 156
2 teaspoons cornstarch
1 cup cooking liquid from Wok Roast,
   page 46, or 1/2 cup Beef Broth and
   1/2 cup Chicken Broth, pages 152-153

1 zucchini
1 carrot
4 oz. cellophane noodles
2 teaspoons peanut oil or vegetable oil
1 onion, chopped
4 oz. fresh or frozen edible pea pods
1 cup shredded Chinese cabbage or
   green cabbage
3 radishes, thinly sliced
1/2 cup sliced green-onion tops

Place beef in a long, shallow dish; add garlic and gingerroot. In a small bowl, stir together sesame oil, soy sauce, sugar, red-pepper flakes and 5-spice powder; pour mixture over beef. Cover and refrigerate 1 hour. In a small bowl, stir together cornstarch and broth until smooth; set aside. Cut zucchini and carrot into thin lengthwise slices; cut slices into strips. Break noodles into 3- to 4-inch lengths. In a large saucepan, bring 3 to 4 quarts water to a boil; add noodles. Cook according to package directions until tender but firm to the bite. While noodles cook, drain meat, reserving marinade; blot meat dry with paper towels. Place wok over high heat; add oil. When hot, add onion, carrot and zucchini; stir-fry 2 minutes or until crisp-tender. Add marinated beef strips; stir-fry 30 seconds. Add pea pods and cabbage; cover and steam 30 seconds. Stir in cornstarch mixture and meat marinade; stir until bubbly hot and slightly thickened. Stir in radishes and green-onion tops. Drain cooked noodles. Serve beef mixture over hot noodles. Makes 4 servings.

About 290 calories per serving.

East-West Stir-Fry

All the meaty flavor you deserve without extra calories.

8 oz. firm tofu, rinsed, drained,
  blotted dry
1/2 lb. lean ground beef
2 teaspoons peanut oil or vegetable oil
1 small onion, chopped
2 celery stalks, cut in thin diagonal slices
1 carrot, cut in paper-thin strips
1/4 lb. young green beans, sliced lengthwise
1 small turnip, thinly sliced,
  then slices cut in wedges

4 large mushrooms, thinly sliced
1/4 cup daikon-radish cubes
1/2 cup diced jícama
1/2 cup Beef Broth, page 152,
  canned broth or water
1 teaspoon honey
3 tablespoons soy sauce
8 oz. fresh spinach, rinsed, blotted dry
1 cup hot cooked ice
1 tablespoon thinly sliced green-onion tops

In a medium bowl, flake tofu with a fork. Add ground beef; stir to blend. Shape mixture into 1 large patty. Place wok over high heat; add oil. When hot, add beef patty; cook 1 to 1-1/2 minutes on each side. Break patty into chunks; stir-fry 1 minute. Add onion, celery, carrot, beans, turnip, mushrooms, radish and jícama; stir-fry 1 minute. Pour in broth or water; reduce heat to medium. Cover and steam 1 minute. Stir in honey and 2 tablespoons soy sauce. Place spinach on top of meat and vegetables. Cover and steam 1 minute. Stir spinach and rice into vegetable mixture. Serve hot, sprinkled with green-onion tops and remaining 1 tablespoon soy sauce. Makes 4 servings.

About 290 calories per serving.

Hawaiian Beef Stir-Fry

Candied ginger adds a sweet accent to this island-style stir-fry.

4 oz. firm tofu, rinsed, drained,
  blotted dry
1 egg
1/4 cup water
2 tablespoons soy sauce
1 teaspoon sesame oil
1/2 lb. lean ground beef
1/2 lb. large mushrooms, quartered

1 small onion, chopped
1 oz. candied ginger, finely chopped
2 tablespoons Beef Broth, page 152,
  canned broth or water
1 cup mung bean sprouts, rinsed,
  drained, blotted dry
2 cups hot cooked rice
1 tablespoon thinly sliced green onion

Cut tofu into 1/2-inch cubes. In a small bowl, beat together egg, water and soy sauce; set aside. Place wok over high heat; add oil. When hot, add ground beef, mushrooms and onion; stir-fry until beef is lightly browned. Stir in tofu cubes and ginger; sprinkle with broth or water. Stir-fry 30 seconds. Cover and steam about 1 minute. Stir in bean sprouts and egg mixture; stir-fry 1 minute. Serve over hot cooked rice. Garnish with green onion. Makes 4 servings.

About 320 calories per serving.

How to Make East-West Stir-Fry

1/Rinse tofu under cold water; drain well. Blot dry with paper towels.

2/ In a medium bowl, flake tofu with a fork.

Meatballs, Vegetables & Noodles

Poaching meatballs in a flavorful broth helps keep the calorie count low.

3/4 lb. lean ground veal
1 egg white
2 tablespoons fine dry bread crumbs or
   cracker crumbs
2 teaspoons soy sauce
2 teaspoons fresh lemon juice
1 teaspoon Oriental chili sauce with garlic
   or 1 teaspoon pure chili powder

1 teaspoon Oriental fish sauce, if desired
2-1/4 teaspoons peanut oil or vegetable oil
1 (8-oz.) pkg. flat spinach noodles
Beef Broth, page 152, canned broth or water
1 small onion, chopped
1 red bell pepper, cut in thin strips
1 green bell pepper, cut in thin strips
4 large mushrooms, coarsely chopped

In a large bowl, combine veal and egg white; knead with your fingers until egg white has been absorbed. Work in crumbs; add soy sauce, lemon juice, chili sauce or chili powder, and fish sauce, if desired. Blend well; form into 16 walnut-sized balls. In a large saucepan, bring 3 to 4 quarts water to a boil. Add 1/4 teaspoon oil and noodles; cook according to package directions until tender but firm to the bite. While pasta cooks, fill wok 1/2 full with broth or water; bring to a simmer. Place meatballs, 1 at a time, in boiling liquid, not crowding the wok. Boil, turning as needed, until cooked through center, about 10 minutes. Remove with a slotted spoon; set aside. Repeat with remaining meatballs. Pour out poaching liquid; wipe wok clean with paper towels. Place wok over high heat. Add remaining 2 teaspoons oil. When hot, add onion, bell peppers and mushrooms; stir-fry 1 to 2 minutes or until crisp-tender. Drain cooked pasta; add to wok along with meatballs; stir over medium heat until heated through. Serve immediately. Makes 4 servings.

About 180 calories per serving.

Veal Scallops Normandy

Cook veal scallops quickly or they will become tough and dry.

8 fresh pearl onions
2 large carrots, thinly sliced
1 small turnip, diced
1 cucumber, peeled, halved lengthwise,
   seeded, cut in thick slices

2 teaspoons peanut oil or vegetable oil
8 (1-1/2-oz.) veal scallops
1/2 teaspoon paprika, if desired

Normandy Sauce:
1 tart apple, peeled, quartered
1 to 2 tablespoons lemon juice
1/4 cup Chicken Broth, page 153,
   canned broth or water

1/4 teaspoon curry powder, if desired
Salt
Freshly ground black pepper

For sauce, in a blender or food processor fitted with a metal blade, combine apple and lemon juice; process to a smooth puree. Transfer to a medium saucepan; stir in broth or water. Stir over medium heat until hot. Stir in curry powder, if desired. Season to taste with salt and pepper. Keep warm until ready to use.

For veal, in a small saucepan of water, boil unpeeled onions 3 minutes. Rinse in cold water and drain. Cut off end of each onion; squeeze to slip off skin. Place peeled onions in a shallow steaming dish. Place dish on a rack in a wok over simmering water; cover and steam 5 minutes. Add carrot slices to dish; cover and steam 5 minutes. Add turnip; cover and steam 5 minutes. Add cucumber crescents; cover and steam 2 minutes or until all vegetables are crisp-tender. Remove vegetables from wok; set aside. Clean and dry wok with paper towels. Place wok over medium-high heat. When hot, add oil and veal scallops; cook 1-1/2 to 2 minutes on each side or until lightly browned. Drain cooked veal on paper towels; place on a platter. Surround with vegetables; pour sauce over top. Sprinkle with paprika, if desired. Makes 4 servings.

About 190 calories per serving.

Veal Scallopini Picata

A delicious variation of an Italian classic.

2 carrots
2 turnips
16 fresh pearl onions
3 teaspoons peanut oil or vegetable oil
2 small cucumbers, peeled,
   halved lengthwise, seeded,
   cut in 1/4-inch-thick slices
1/4 cup Vegetable Broth, page 152, or water

1 teaspoon sugar
8 (1-1/2-oz.) veal scallops
2 tablespoons dry white wine
2 tablespoons fresh lemon juice
Salt
Freshly ground black pepper
1 tablespoon minced fresh parsley

Cut carrots and turnips in small oval shapes of equal size. In a small saucepan of water, boil unpeeled onions 3 minutes. Rinse in cold water and drain. Cut off end of each onion; squeeze to slip off skin. Place wok over medium heat; add 1 teaspoon oil. When hot, add carrot and turnip ovals, cucumber slices and peeled onions; stir-fry about 1 minute. Pour in broth or water; cover and steam 2 minutes or until vegetables are easily pierced. Increase heat to high; stirring frequently, boil until liquid is reduced to about 2 tablespoons. Stir in sugar; stir-fry until vegetables are lightly glazed. Transfer to a bowl; keep vegetables warm. Clean wok; wipe dry with paper towels. Place wok over high heat; add remaining 2 teaspoons oil. Add veal; cook 1 minute on each side. Add wine and lemon juice; bring to a full boil. Season to taste with salt and pepper. Place 2 veal scallops on each of 4 warmed plates. Spoon sauce over each. Sprinkle with parsley. Surround with cooked vegetables. Makes 4 servings.

About 170 calories per serving.

Veal scallops are small, lean pieces of veal loin or sirloin.

How to Make Lamb Chops with Mustard Sauce

1/For each packet, arrange lamb slices, slightly overlapping on foil. Arrange grapes and tomatoes around lamb slices. Season to taste. Spoon sauce over top.

2/ Place sealed packets on a rack in a wok over simmering water; cover and steam 5 minutes or until heated through.

Lamb Chops with Mustard Sauce

These silvery packets are opened at the table, releasing their savory fragrance.

**2 lean boneless lamb loin chops,
  1-1/2 inches thick
1/4 lb. seedless green grapes,
  broken in small clusters
8 cherry tomatoes
Salt**

**Freshly ground black pepper
1 tablespoon white-wine vinegar or
  tarragon vinegar
2 tablespoons Dijon-style mustard
1 teaspoon sugar**

Place chops on a rack in a wok over simmering water; cover and steam 10 to 12 minutes. Transfer chops to a cutting board; cover and let stand 10 to 15 minutes to cool. Cut 2 (12-inch-square) foil pieces. Cut chops crosswise into 1/2-inch-thick slices. For 1 packet, arrange 1/2 of lamb slices, slightly overlapping, on a foil piece. Arrange 1/2 of grapes and 4 tomatoes around lamb slices. Season to taste with salt and pepper. Repeat for other packet. In a small bowl, stir together vinegar, mustard and sugar; spoon 1/2 of mixture over center of lamb slices for each packet. Bring sides of each foil piece up toward center; seal with a drug-store fold, leaving sufficient room for steaming, page 87. Place sealed packets on a rack in a wok over simmering water; cover and steam 5 minutes or until heated through. Transfer each packet to a serving plate. Makes 2 servings.

About 180 calories per serving.

Wok Roast

Great the first time as well as to use leftovers for a quick stir-fry.

1 (4-lb.) beef sirloin-tip roast
1 teaspoon peanut oil or vegetable oil
1-1/2 teaspoons Quatre Epices, page 155

1 tablespoon soy sauce
1 teaspoon freshly ground black pepper
1/4 teaspoon salt

Place roast on a large piece of heavy foil. Using your hands, rub roast with oil, spices, soy sauce, pepper and salt. Wrap roast tightly in foil to seal in juices. Refrigerate foil-wrapped roast 12 to 24 hours. Place foil-wrapped roast on a rack in a wok over simmering water. Cover and steam 2 to 3 hours or to desired doneness, adding water to wok as needed. Remove from wok; let stand 10 minutes. Open foil over a bowl to catch all cooking juices. Place roast on a cutting surface; discard foil. Cut roast crosswise into thin slices. Arrange slices, slightly overlapping, in a shallow baking dish. Pour cooking juices over surface. Cover and refrigerate several hours, allowing meat to absorb juices and flavor. To serve, remove and discard any congealed fat. Reheat slices in juice; serve hot. Or, arrange cold slices on a serving plate. Makes 14 servings.

About 200 calories per serving.

Chinese Red-Braised Pork

This pork is flamed in bourbon, then simmered in a tasty blend of apple juice and chili sauce.

1 (1-3/4- to 2-lb.) pork tenderloin
1 tablespoon Oriental chili sauce
   with garlic
1-1/2 cups unsweetened apple juice

1/4 cup soy sauce
3 to 4 drops red food coloring, if desired
2 teaspoons peanut oil or vegetable oil
1/4 cup bourbon whiskey

Place pork in a long, shallow dish; spread with chili sauce. In a medium bowl, stir together apple juice, soy sauce and food coloring, if desired; pour over pork. Cover and refrigerate several hours, turning pork occasionally. To cook, remove pork from marinade, reserving marinade; blot dry with paper towels. Place wok over high heat; add oil. When hot, add pork; brown quickly on all sides, turning with tongs to avoid piercing the meat. Add bourbon; using a long match, carefully ignite bourbon. Let flame burn briefly, then extinguish by adding reserved marinade. Reduce heat to low; cover and simmer, turning occasionally, 40 to 45 minutes or until pork reaches 165F (75C) on a meat thermometer. Transfer pork to a cutting surface, reserving cooking liquid. Cover and cool 10 to 15 minutes. Cut pork crosswise into thin slices. Arrange slices, slightly overlapping, in a shallow dish. Pour reserved cooking liquid over slices. Cover and refrigerate several hours or until ready to use, turning slices in marinade occasionally. Serve as part of a cold Chinese-style buffet or use in other stir-fry dishes. Makes 8 servings.

About 230 calories per serving.

Stir-Fried Pork & Pea Pods

A delicious combination of color, texture and taste.

1/2 lb. lean boneless pork,
   cut in thin strips
1 tablespoon soy sauce
2 tablespoons dry sherry
1/2 teaspoon sugar
2 teaspoons peanut oil or vegetable oil
1/4 cup Vegetable Broth or Chicken Broth,
   pages 152-153, canned broth or water

1/2 lb. fresh edible pea pods or
   1 (10-oz.) pkg. frozen pea pods
1 cup mung bean sprouts, rinsed,
   drained, blotted dry
1/2 cup pimento strips
2 cups hot cooked rice
Additional soy sauce, if desired

Place pork strips in a long, shallow dish; sprinkle with 1 tablespoon soy sauce, sherry and sugar. Cover and refrigerate 30 minutes. Remove strips from marinade, reserving marinade; blot dry with paper towels. Place wok over high heat; add oil. When hot, add marinated pork; stir-fry until lightly browned. Pour in broth or water. Reduce heat to medium-low; cover and simmer 20 minutes. Then stir-fry until liquid evaporates. Stir in reserved marinade and pea pods; stir-fry 2 minutes. Stir in bean sprouts and pimento; stir-fry 1 minute. Serve over hot cooked rice with additional soy sauce, if desired. Makes 4 servings.

About 270 calories per serving.

Pork & Vegetables in Mustard Cream

A hearty German-style dish with a low-calorie sauce.

2 potatoes, peeled, diced
1 small turnip, diced
2 large carrots, diced
1 green bell pepper, cut in thin strips
2 tablespoons evaporated skim milk
2 tablespoons water
2 tablespoons Dijon-style mustard
2 teaspoons cornstarch

2 teaspoons peanut oil or vegetable oil
3/4 lb. pork tenderloin, cut in thin slices
2 tablespoons white-wine vinegar
1 cup Chicken Broth or Vegetable Broth,
   pages 152-153, canned broth or water
Salt
Freshly ground black pepper
Minced fresh dill or green-onion tops

Place potatoes, turnip and carrots in a steamer dish on a rack in a wok over simmering water; cover and steam 10 minutes or until tender. Add bell pepper; steam 1 minute. Set steamed vegetables aside. In a small bowl, combine milk, 2 tablespoons water, mustard and cornstarch. Place wok over high heat; add oil. When hot, add pork slices; stir-fry until lightly browned. Add vinegar; stir to deglaze wok. Pour in broth or water; bring to a boil. Reduce heat: cover and steam 5 minutes. Stir in milk mixture and steamed vegetables; cook, stirring frequently, until liquid is slightly thickened. Season with salt and pepper. Garnish with dill or green-onion tops. Makes 4 servings.

About 250 calories per serving.

Polynesian-Style Pork with Vegetables

A taste straight from the islands.

1/2 small bunch broccoli, about 1/4 lb.
1 (8-oz.) can pineapple chunks in
  unsweetened juice
2 tablespoons soy sauce
1/2 cup water
2 teaspoons cornstarch
2 teaspoons peanut oil or vegetable oil
1 small garlic clove, crushed
1 (1-inch) piece gingerroot, crushed
1 small onion, chopped
2 celery stalks, cut diagonally
  in thin slices
1 small red bell pepper,
  cut in 1-inch squares

2 tablespoons marinade from
  Chinese Red-Braised Pork, page 46;
  Chicken Broth, page 153;
  or canned broth
1/2 lb. Chinese Red-Braised Pork, page 46,
  cut in 1/2-inch cubes,
  or 1/2 lb. other cooked pork
1 cup shredded bok choy or Chinese cabbage
1 small jícama, cut in thin strips
1 tablespoon grated radish or daikon radish
2 cups hot cooked rice

Break broccoli into flowerets; rinse and drain well. Blot dry with paper towels. Trim broccoli stems; cut in thin strips. Drain pineapple, reserving juice. In a small bowl, stir together pineapple juice, soy sauce, water and cornstarch until smooth; set aside. Place wok over high heat; add oil. When hot, add garlic and gingerroot; stir-fry until lightly browned. Remove and discard garlic and gingerroot. Add onion, celery, bell pepper and broccoli stems to wok; stir-fry 1 minute. Sprinkle with marinade or broth; cover and steam 30 seconds. Add broccoli flowerets and pork; stir-fry 1 minute. Stir cornstarch mixture into pork mixture; cook, stirring constantly, until sauce is slightly thickened. Stir in bok choy or Chinese cabbage, pineapple, jícama and radish. Stir until mixture is heated through. Serve over hot cooked rice. Makes 4 servings.

About 320 calories per serving.

POULTRY & EGGS

Chicken is low in calories and is an important ingredient in any calorie-cutting plan. To cut calories even more, remove skin and excess fat from chicken. Chicken breast or white meat is lower in calories than dark meat. For that reason, you will find many recipes for skinned, boneless chicken breasts in this chapter.

Chicken has superb flavor and it offers endless possibilities for blending with other foods. Chicken can be cooked quickly with a variety of seasonings and sauces. Team it up with colorful, crunchy vegetables to satisfy that hardy appetite. Serve chicken over rice, pasta or vegetables. And, there you are, a variety of totally different but equally delicious, low-calorie, satisfying meals.

Turkey is a versatile, low-calorie meat. It is now available year-round in a variety of forms, including whole breast, half breast, turkey breast slices, turkey quarters, turkey legs and ground turkey. Look for turkey products in your fresh-meat case or in the frozen-meat section. An excellent meat value is ground turkey. It is lower in both price and calories than other ground meats. Try substituting ground turkey for other ground meats in some of your favorite recipes.

Although a traditional breakfast food, eggs answer the need for a low-calorie food any time of day. Eggs can be cooked in a variety of ways and combinations with other foods and seasonings.

Menu

Breakfast
1 English muffin   1 oz. Neufchâtel cheese
Grapefruit juice
Coffee or tea

Snack
Coffee or tea   3 crackers

Lunch
Terrific Turkey Salad, page 118
1 slice whole-wheat bread   1 oz. Neufchâtel cheese
1/2 cup sliced cucumbers
Diet soda

Dinner
Turkey Chili Con Carne, page 68
Pears in Raspberry Glaze, page 135
Coffee or tea

Snack
1 cup unbuttered popcorn

About 1200 calories

Deviled Chicken Strips

Guests of all ages will enjoy these tangy chicken strips.

2 Swedish-style bran fiber bread crackers
1 tablespoon Dijon-style mustard
2 or 3 dashes hot-pepper sauce
1 tablespoon fresh lemon juice
1/8 teaspoon salt

1/8 teaspoon freshly ground black pepper
3/4 cup Chicken Broth, page 153,
  canned broth or water
4 boneless chicken-breast halves, skinned

In a blender or food processor fitted with a metal blade, crush crackers to fine crumbs. Spread crumbs on waxed paper or a flat surface; set aside. In a large shallow bowl, combine mustard, hot-pepper sauce, lemon juice, salt, black pepper and 1/2 cup broth or water; set aside. Place wok over high heat. When hot, add chicken pieces. Cook 1 minute or until lightly browned; turn and cook 1 minute or until browned. Reduce heat; add remaining 1/4 cup broth or water. Cover and steam 1 minute. Uncover and cook, turning breast pieces occasionally, until liquid has evaporated and chicken is firm and white through center. Transfer cooked chicken to a cutting surface; cut into lengthwise 1/2-inch strips. Dip each chicken strip in mustard mixture, then roll in crumbs. Any remaining crumbs and mustard mixture may be sprinkled over top. Serve at room temperature. Makes 4 servings.

About 220 calories per serving.

Stir-Fried Chicken San Marco

An Italian dish, cooked on the light side.

1 lb. chicken thighs, boned, skinned
1/2 teaspoon dried leaf oregano
1/4 teaspoon dried leaf basil
Salt
Freshly ground black pepper
2 teaspoons peanut oil or vegetable oil
2 to 3 garlic cloves, minced

3 tablespoons red-wine vinegar
1 (16-oz.) can peeled tomatoes, crushed,
  reserving juice
2 cups hot cooked rice
1 tablespoon minced chives
1 tablespoon minced parsley
1 tablespoon grated Parmesan cheese

Using the flat side of a cleaver or meat mallet, pound chicken until flattened; dice chicken. Sprinkle chicken with oregano, basil, 1/8 teaspoon salt and 1/8 teaspoon pepper; press seasonings into chicken. Place wok over high heat; add oil. When hot, add seasoned chicken; stir-fry 2 minutes. Add garlic; stir-fry 30 seconds. Add vinegar; boil until liquid has evaporated. Add tomatoes and 1/2 cup reserved juice to wok. Reduce heat and simmer 5 minutes or until chicken is cooked through. Season to taste with salt and pepper. Serve over hot cooked rice. Garnish with chives, parsley and cheese. Makes 4 servings.

About 290 calories per serving.

Cuban-Style Stir-Fried Chicken

Artichoke hearts add special flavor and pimento strips give color to this recipe.

1 teaspoon chili powder
Salt
1 teaspoon cornstarch
1/4 cup fresh orange juice
1 cup Vegetable Broth or Chicken Broth,
   pages 152-153, canned broth or water
1 lb. chicken thighs, boned, skinned

2 teaspoons peanut oil or vegetable oil
1 (10-oz.) pkg. thawed frozen artichoke
   hearts, quartered
1/2 cup drained pimento strips
Freshly ground black pepper
2 cups hot cooked rice

In a small bowl, combine chili powder, 1/4 teaspoon salt and cornstarch; stir in orange juice and 1/2 cup broth or water. Set mixture aside. Using the flat side of a cleaver or meat mallet, pound chicken until flattened; cut into narrow strips. Place wok over high heat; add oil. When hot, add chicken strips; stir-fry until cooked through. Sprinkle with remaining 1/2 cup broth or water; cover and steam 30 seconds. Uncover and stir-fry until liquid has evaporated. Stir cornstarch mixture into wok; cook, stirring constantly, until slightly thickened. Stir in artichokes and pimentos; cook until heated through. Season to taste with salt and pepper. Serve over hot cooked rice. Makes 4 servings.

About 290 calories per serving.

Caribbean Chicken with Shrimp & Ham

This typical island dish is filled with a blend of flavors.

1 lb. chicken thighs, boned, skinned
2 teaspoons peanut oil or vegetable oil
1 onion, chopped
1 green bell pepper, diced
1 garlic clove, minced
1/2 teaspoon turmeric
1/4 teaspoon dried leaf oregano
1/4 teaspoon dried leaf coriander
1/2 teaspoon salt

1/4 teaspoon freshly ground black pepper
1 (12-oz.) can stewed tomatoes
1 oz. lean cooked ham, cut in thin strips
1/4 lb. large shrimp, peeled, deveined,
   coarsely chopped
1/2 cup thawed frozen green peas
4 small pimento-stuffed green olives, sliced
1 tablespoon capers, drained, if desired
1 cup shredded lettuce

Using the flat side of a cleaver or meat mallet, pound chicken until flattened; cut into narrow strips. Place wok over high heat; add oil. When hot, add onion and bell pepper; stir-fry 1 minute. Add chicken strips; stir-fry until cooked through. Stir in garlic, turmeric, oregano, coriander, salt and black pepper; stir-fry 30 seconds. Add stewed tomatoes. Reduce heat and cover; simmer 2 to 3 minutes. Add ham and shrimp; stir-fry until shrimp is pink. Add peas and olives; stir-fry 1 minute. Add capers, if desired. Serve hot over shredded lettuce. Makes 4 servings.

About 230 calories per serving.

Chicken with Green Beans

This is an easy stir-fry recipe you will prepare often.

1/2 lb. boneless chicken-breast halves,
  skinned
1 teaspoon cornstarch
1/2 cup Vegetable Broth or Chicken Broth,
  pages 152-153, canned broth or water
1 tablespoon soy sauce
1/2 teaspoon sesame oil

4 teaspoons peanut oil or vegetable oil
1/2 lb. young green beans
1/4 lb. mushrooms, sliced
1 (8-oz.) can bamboo shoots, drained
Freshly ground black pepper
2 cups hot cooked rice

Using the flat side of a cleaver or meat mallet, pound chicken pieces until flattened; cut in 1/4-inch strips. In a small bowl, stir together cornstarch and broth or water; stir in soy sauce and sesame oil. Set mixture aside. Place wok over high heat; add 3 teaspoons peanut oil or vegetable oil. When hot, add beans; stir-fry 3 to 4 minutes. Add mushrooms; stir-fry 1 to 2 minutes or until beans and mushrooms are crisp-tender. Transfer to a small bowl; keep warm. Add remaining 1 teaspoon oil to wok. When hot, add chicken strips; stir-fry until firm and white through center. Add cooked beans, mushrooms, bamboo shoots and cornstarch mixture to wok; stir until slightly thickened. Season to taste with pepper. Serve over hot cooked rice. Makes 4 servings.

About 270 calories per serving.

Garlicky Orange Chicken

If you grow your own herbs, substitute fresh herbs for dried.

1 orange
2 teaspoons peanut oil or vegetable oil
1 lb. chicken thighs, boned, skinned, diced
2 tablespoons cider vinegar
1/4 cup fresh orange juice
1/4 cup water
1 large garlic clove, minced

1 (1/2-inch) piece gingerroot, minced
1/2 teaspoon dried leaf basil, crushed
1/4 teaspoon dried leaf oregano, crushed
1/8 teaspoon dried rosemary, crushed
Salt
Freshly ground black pepper
2 cups hot cooked rice

Peel orange, removing all white pith; cut in quarter wedges, reserving juice. Place wok over high heat; add oil. When hot, add chicken; stir-fry 2 minutes or until cooked through. Pour in vinegar, orange juice and water; sprinkle with garlic, gingerroot, basil, oregano and rosemary. Reduce heat; cover and simmer 3 minutes. Season to taste with salt and pepper. Stir-fry until nearly all liquid has evaporated. Serve over hot cooked rice. Makes 4 servings.

About 180 calories per serving.

How to Make Chicken with Shiitake Mushrooms

1/Drain mushrooms, reserving water. Remove tough stems from mushrooms.

2/Cut mushrooms in thin, even strips.

Chicken with Shiitake Mushrooms

Dried shiitake mushrooms and Madeira add a delightful flavor to chicken.

1 lb. chicken thighs, boned, skinned
1 tablespoon soy sauce
2 tablespoons Madeira
4 large dried shiitake mushrooms
3/4 cup warm water
2 teaspoons peanut oil or vegetable oil
4 small dried red chilies
1 (1-inch) piece gingerroot, minced

1 small garlic clove, minced
1 small red bell pepper, cut in thin strips
1 (8-oz.) can bamboo shoots, drained,
  cut in thin strips
1 tablespoon hoisin sauce
2 cups hot cooked rice
2 tablespoons thinly sliced green onion

Using the flat side of a cleaver or meat mallet, pound chicken until flattened; dice chicken. In a medium bowl, combine diced chicken, soy sauce and Madeira; let stand 30 minutes. In a small bowl, combine mushrooms and warm water; let stand 30 minutes. Drain mushrooms, reserving water. Remove tough stems. Cut mushrooms in thin strips. Place wok over high heat; add oil. When hot, add chilies; stir-fry 30 seconds or until browned. Remove and discard chilies. Add gingerroot and garlic to wok; stir-fry 30 seconds. Add bell pepper; stir-fry until crisp-tender. Drain chicken, reserving marinade; add chicken to wok. Stir-fry until chicken is cooked through. Add reserved marinade and water from mushrooms; boil until nearly all liquid has evaporated. Stir in mushrooms and bamboo shoots; stir-fry 30 seconds. Add hoisin sauce; stir until heated through. Serve over hot cooked rice. Garnish with green onion. Makes 4 servings.

About 310 calories per serving.

How to Make Chicken with Dipping Sauces

1/Using your fingers or a spatula, force a lemon slice under breast skin on each side.

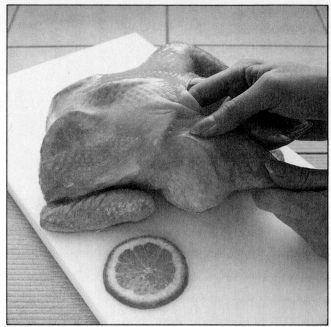

2/Force 2 remaining lemon slices under skin of each leg and thigh, being careful not to tear the skin.

Chicken with Avgolemono Sauce

Avgolemono sauce is a Greek sauce made with lemon juice and egg yolks.

8 chicken thighs, skinned
1 teaspoon peanut oil or vegetable oil
1 small onion, minced
6 mushrooms, minced
1 celery stalk, chopped
3 cups Chicken Broth, page 153,
   canned broth or water
1/2 teaspoon salt

1/8 teaspoon freshly ground black pepper
1 bay leaf
2 tablespoons water
2 teaspoons cornstarch
2 egg yolks
1/4 cup fresh lemon juice
Paprika

Remove any excess fat from chicken. Place wok over medium heat; add oil. When hot, add onion, mushrooms and celery; stir-fry until crisp-tender. Add broth or water; bring to a simmer. Add chicken, salt, pepper and bay leaf; simmer 25 minutes or until chicken is tender and cooked through. Remove chicken; cover and keep warm. Simmer stock until reduced to about 1-3/4 cups; strain through a fine sieve into a medium saucepan. In a small bowl, stir together water and cornstarch until smooth. In a medium bowl, beat egg yolks until light and lemon colored. Slowly beat in lemon juice. Add cornstarch mixture to strained broth, stirring until smooth. Place saucepan over medium heat; bring to a simmer, stirring frequently until slightly thickened. Remove from heat; stir in egg mixture. Season to taste with salt and pepper. Spoon sauce over chicken; sprinkle with paprika. Makes 4 servings.

About 230 calories per serving.

Fragrant Chicken with Dipping Sauces

You will need a wok with a domed lid for cooking this whole chicken.

1 (3- to 3-1/2-lb.) chicken
Salt
1 tablespoon minced gingerroot
1 tablespoon minced garlic

1/2 small lemon, unpeeled, chopped
4 thin lemon slices
2 tablespoons sherry-wine vinegar
1/4 cup honey

Soy-Sauce Dip:
1/4 cup soy sauce
2 tablespoons fresh lemon juice

1 tablespoon Oriental plum sauce,
   if desired

Sweet & Sour Dip:
2 tablespoons dry mustard
1 tablespoon sugar
2 tablespoons rice-wine vinegar or
   sherry-wine vinegar

1/4 cup Chicken Broth or Vegetable Broth,
   pages 152-153, canned broth or water

Hot-Pepper Dip:
2 tablespoons peanut oil or
   vegetable oil
2 teaspoons sesame oil
1 teaspoon minced garlic
1 teaspoon Oriental peppercorns
1 tablespoon minced gingerroot

1 tablespoon chopped hot red chili peppers
2 tablespoons rice-wine vinegar or
   sherry-wine vinegar
1 teaspoon sugar
Salt

Rinse chicken under cold running water; blot dry with paper towels. Season inside chicken with 1 teaspoon salt. Place gingerroot, garlic and chopped lemon in chicken body cavity. Starting at the breast, separate skin from meat of chicken by gently pushing your fingers between skin and chicken, being careful not to puncture skin. Using a rubber spatula or your fingers, force 2 lemon slices under breast skin; force 2 remaining lemon slices under skin of each leg. Place chicken in a shallow steaming dish; place on a rack in a wok over simmering water. Cover and steam 20 to 25 minutes or until juices run clear when a knife is inserted between thigh and breast. Insert a wooden spoon in chicken cavity; lift chicken and let juices drain into steaming dish. Transfer chicken to a large bowl; let stand until cool enough to handle. Strain juices from steaming dish through a fine sieve into a large bowl. Remove and discard skin from cooked chicken. Pull chicken in large pieces from bones, discarding bones. Add cooked chicken to reserved juices. In a 1-cup measure, combine vinegar and honey; blend well. Pour over chicken pieces; toss to coat.

To serve, arrange chicken pieces in an attractive design on a platter. Serve warm or at room temperature with desired dipping sauces. Makes 5 servings.

For soy-sauce dip and sweet & sour dip, in small bowls, blend ingredients for each dip.

For hot-pepper dip, place wok over medium heat; add peanut oil or vegetable oil and sesame oil. When hot, add garlic, peppercorns, gingerroot and chili peppers; stir until ginger and garlic are golden. Remove wok from heat. Cool, then strain oil into a small bowl; discard seasonings. Stir vinegar and sugar into oil. Season to taste with salt. Serve hot or at room temperature.

About 350 calories per serving for chicken, 12 calories per tablespoon Soy-Sauce Dip, 14 calories per tablespoon Sweet & Sour Dip, and 70 calories per tablespoon Hot-Pepper Dip.

Chicken Puffs with Plum Sauce

Great idea for a Sunday brunch.

Plum Sauce:

1 (8-oz.) can unsweetened whole
   purple plums

2 teaspoons prepared horseradish

Chicken Puffs:

1/4 cup minced celery
1/4 cup minced green or red bell pepper
1/4 cup thinly sliced green onions
1 tablespoon minced radish or daikon radish
1 tablespoon finely chopped sweet pickle
1 cup finely shredded cooked chicken

2 eggs, separated
About 1 teaspoon soy sauce
2 or 3 drops sesame oil, if desired
Dash of Chinese Five-Spice Powder,
   page 156, if desired
2 teaspoons peanut oil or vegetable oil

For sauce, drain and pit plums. In a medium bowl, mash plums to a chunky sauce; stir in horseradish. Refrigerate or serve at room temperature.

For puffs, in a large bowl, combine celery, bell pepper, green onions, radish, pickle and chicken; blend well. Stir in egg yolks. Season with soy sauce and sesame oil, if desired. Add 5-spice powder. In another bowl, beat egg whites until soft peaks form. Fold into chicken mixture, blending well. Lightly oil bottom of wok; place over medium heat. When oil is hot, spoon a scant 1/4 cup chicken mixture into wok; repeat for 2 more puffs. Cook 2 to 3 minutes or until lightly browned on underside and dry through center; turn with a spatula and lightly brown other side. Transfer to a warm plate. Repeat with remaining batter, adding oil to wok as needed. Sprinkle puffs with additional soy sauce, if desired. Serve chicken puffs with plum sauce. Makes 4 servings.

About 160 calories per serving.

Grilled Chicken Piquant

These quick, low-calorie chicken breasts have unbelievable flavor—try them for yourself!

2 boneless chicken-breast halves, skinned
Salt
1/4 cup dry white wine or vermouth

2 tablespoons fresh lemon juice
Freshly ground black pepper

Using the flat side of a cleaver or meat mallet, pound each chicken piece until evenly thin and about doubled in size; pat dry with paper towels. Place wok over high heat; sprinkle lightly with salt. When hot, salt will darken slightly. Add chicken pieces, cooking 1 minute or until lightly browned; turn and cook 1 minute. Add wine or vermouth; cover and steam 1 minute. Reduce heat. Uncover and cook until firm and white through center. Sprinkle with lemon juice; season to taste with salt and pepper. Serve immediately. Makes 2 servings.

About 170 calories per serving.

Chicken-Breast Florentine

Steamed to perfection.

2 boneless chicken-breast halves, skinned
8 to 12 large spinach leaves, stems removed
1 teaspoon currant jelly
About 1 teaspoon soy sauce

About 2 teaspoons fresh lemon juice
4 thin lemon slices
1 small garlic clove, minced
Freshly ground black pepper

Using the flat side of a cleaver or meat mallet, pound chicken until flattened. Cut 2 (12-inch-square) foil pieces. Arrange spinach on foil pieces, dividing evenly. Place chicken breasts over spinach; spread each with jelly. Sprinkle with soy sauce and lemon juice. Arrange 2 lemon slices over each chicken breast. Sprinkle lightly with garlic and pepper. Bring sides of each foil piece up toward center; seal with a drug-store fold, leaving sufficient room for steaming, page 87. Place sealed packets on a rack in a wok over simmering water. Cover wok and steam 20 minutes, adding water to wok as needed. Chicken should be firm and white through center. Transfer packets to a platter. Serve immediately. Makes 2 servings.

About 170 calories per serving.

Chicken with Red Cabbage

A flavorful version of a favorite recipe.

2 teaspoons cornstarch
2 teaspoons brown sugar
1/4 cup soy sauce
1/4 cup rice wine or dry sherry
2 teaspoons white-wine vinegar
About 2/3 cup Chicken Broth or
   Vegetable Broth, pages 152-153,
   canned broth or water
1/8 teaspoon garlic salt
1/8 teaspoon red (cayenne) pepper

1/8 teaspoon freshly ground black pepper
1 lb. boneless chicken-breast halves,
   skinned
2 teaspoons peanut oil or vegetable oil
1 small red bell pepper, cut in thin strips
1/2 small red cabbage, finely shredded,
   about 2 cups
1/4 cup thinly sliced green onions
2 tablespoons sesame seeds

In a 2-cup measure, combine cornstarch and brown sugar; stir in soy sauce, rice wine or sherry, vinegar, 1/2 cup broth or water, garlic salt, red pepper and black pepper. Set mixture aside. Using the flat side of a cleaver or meat mallet, pound chicken pieces until flattened; cut into narrow strips. Place wok over high heat; add oil. When hot, add chicken strips; stir-fry about 2 minutes. Add bell pepper; stir-fry 30 seconds. Add cabbage; sprinkle with remaining 2 tablespoons broth or water. Cover and steam 1 minute. Uncover and stir-fry until cabbage is crisp-tender. Stir cornstarch mixture into wok. Cook, stirring frequently, until slightly thickened and chicken is firm and white through center. Add green onions and sesame seeds; toss briefly. Serve immediately. Makes 4 servings.

About 260 calories per serving.

Chicken with Vegetable Rice

Chicken prepared in a wok is juicy and flavorful, and cooks in less than six minutes.

2 boneless chicken-breast halves, skinned
1 small carrot
1 small zucchini
Salt
1 tablespoon fresh lemon juice
2 tablespoons dry white wine or vermouth
1/4 cup Chicken Broth, page 153,
    canned broth or water

Freshly ground black pepper
2 teaspoons peanut oil or vegetable oil
1 teaspoon thinly sliced green onion
1 cup cold cooked rice
Garlic salt

Using the flat side of a cleaver or meat mallet, pound each chicken breast until 1/4 inch thick; blot dry with paper towels. Cut carrot and zucchini lengthwise into thin, 1-inch sticks; set aside. Place wok over high heat; sprinkle bottom evenly with salt. When hot, salt will darken slightly. Add chicken pieces in a single layer; cook 1 minute or until lightly browned. Turn and cook other side. Add lemon juice, wine or vermouth, and broth or water. Cover and steam 1 minute. Uncover and cook until chicken is firm and white through center, and liquid is reduced to about 1 tablespoon. Remove chicken to a plate; sprinkle with remaining liquid. Season to taste with salt and pepper. Keep chicken warm. Heat oil in wok. When hot, add carrot and zucchini strips; stir-fry 1 minute. Add green onion and rice; stir-fry mixture until heated through. Season lightly with garlic salt and pepper. Serve hot with chicken. Makes 2 servings.

About 310 calories per serving.

Poached Chicken with Vegetables & Orzo

Orzo is a small pasta that looks like rice or barley.

4 chicken thighs, skinned
4 chicken legs, skinned
2 cups Chicken Broth, page 153,
    canned broth or water
2 carrots, cut in 1/2-inch slices
2 turnips, diced
2 celery stalks, cut in 1/2-inch slices
1 leek, white part only,
    separated into leaves, thoroughly washed

8 mushrooms
1 teaspoon salt
1/4 teaspoon freshly ground black pepper
1/2 teaspoon dried leaf thyme
2 bay leaves
1/2 cup orzo

Remove any excess fat from chicken. In a wok, combine chicken, broth or water, and carrots. Place over medium heat; bring to a boil. Reduce heat and simmer 10 minutes. Add turnips, celery, leek, mushrooms, salt, pepper, thyme and bay leaves. Cover and simmer 20 minutes. Stir in orzo; cover and simmer 20 minutes or until chicken, vegetables and orzo are tender. Serve in shallow soup bowls. Makes 4 servings.

About 270 calories per serving.

Zucchini & Tomato-Chicken Sauce

A new way to cook zucchini.

4 zucchini, about 1 lb.	Salt
3 large tomatoes, peeled	1/2 teaspoon Italian Seasoning, page 155
2 teaspoons peanut oil or vegetable oil	2 teaspoons white-wine vinegar
1 garlic clove, minced	1 teaspoon sugar
1/4 teaspoon dried red-pepper flakes	1 cup shredded or diced cooked chicken

Cut zucchini lengthwise into 1/4-inch-thick strips. Cut tomatoes into chunks, reserving juice; set aside. Place wok over high heat; add oil. When hot, add 1/2 of zucchini strips; stir-fry 2 minutes. Stir in 1/2 of garlic, 1/8 teaspoon red-pepper flakes and 1/4 teaspoon salt. Stir-fry until zucchini softens. Drain in a sieve over a bowl to collect the oil; keep warm. Return drained oil to wok; add remaining zucchini. Stir-fry 2 minutes. Stir in remaining garlic, red-pepper flakes and 1/4 teaspoon salt; stir-fry until softened. Drain in sieve. Place cooked zucchini on a platter; keep warm. Place tomatoes with juice and Italian Seasoning in wok; stir-fry, breaking up tomatoes until reduced to a thick, chunky sauce. Add vinegar and sugar; stir in chicken. Season to taste with salt. Reduce heat and cover; simmer 2 to 3 minutes. Ladle sauce over cooked zucchini. Makes 4 servings.

About 120 calories per serving.

Chicken with Cilantro

Cilantro is fresh coriander; it adds great flavor to this low-fat fare.

4 boneless chicken-breast halves, skinned	2 tablespoons tomato paste
2 teaspoons peanut oil or vegetable oil	2 cups Vegetable Broth or Chicken Broth,
1 large onion, chopped	pages 152-153, canned broth or water
2 tablespoons finely chopped cilantro	Dash hot-pepper sauce
1 teaspoon curry powder	Salt
1/2 teaspoon dry mustard	Freshly ground black pepper
Pinch of ground cloves	2 cups hot cooked rice

Using the flat side of a cleaver or meat mallet, pound chicken until flattened. Cut chicken into narrow strips; set aside. Place wok over high heat; add oil. When hot, add onion; stir-fry 2 minutes or until crisp-tender. Stir in cilantro and curry powder; stir-fry 30 seconds. Add mustard, cloves, tomato paste and broth or water; bring to a boil. Add chicken strips; stir-fry 2 to 3 minutes. Reduce heat and simmer 10 minutes or until chicken is firm and white through center. Season to taste with hot-pepper sauce, salt and pepper. Serve over hot cooked rice. Makes 4 servings.

About 300 calories per serving.

Simple Chicken Superb

An easy chicken recipe with as much flavor as chicken prepared in grandmother's day.

2 chicken-breast halves,
  2 legs and 2 thighs
2 tablespoons fresh lemon juice
1 garlic clove, crushed
3/4 cup Chicken Broth, page 153,
  canned broth or water

1/2 teaspoon salt
1/4 lb. large mushrooms
Paprika

Remove and discard skin from breast halves; blot dry with paper towels. Place wok over medium heat. Arrange legs and thighs in a single layer, skin-side down, in wok. Cook, without turning, until sufficient fat has been rendered out to allow chicken to move easily in wok. Cook, turning pieces occasionally, until skin is browned. Remove and cool slightly; remove and discard skin. Pour off excess fat. Return wok to medium heat; add chicken pieces. Sprinkle with lemon juice. Add garlic, broth or water and salt. Simmer 20 to 25 minutes or until chicken is firm and cooked through. Add mushrooms; cover and steam 5 minutes. Transfer chicken and mushrooms to a platter. Remove and discard garlic from remaining cooking liquid. Sprinkle remaining liquid over chicken pieces. Sprinkle chicken with paprika. Serve hot or at room temperature. Makes 4 servings.

About 150 calories per serving.

10-Minute Dijon Chicken

A quick dish with exceptional flavor.

1 lb. chicken thighs, boned, skinned
1 tablespoon Dijon-style mustard
1 teaspoon cornstarch
1/4 cup Chicken Broth or Vegetable Broth,
  pages 152-153, canned broth or water
1 teaspoon peanut oil or vegetable oil
1 small green bell pepper,
  cut in thin strips

1 small onion, chopped
2 tablespoons dry white wine
1 (12-oz.) can Italian-style peeled tomatoes
1/4 cup water
1/2 teaspoon Italian Seasoning, page 155
Salt
Freshly ground black pepper
2 cups hot cooked rice

Using the flat side of a cleaver or meat mallet, pound chicken pieces until flattened; cut into narrow strips. In a small bowl, stir together mustard, cornstarch and broth or water until smooth; set aside. Using 1 teaspoon oil, lightly oil bottom and side of wok; place over high heat. When hot, add chicken strips, bell pepper and onion; stir-fry 1 minute. Reduce heat to medium-low. Add wine; bring to a simmer. Crush tomatoes; add to wok with juice, water and Italian Seasoning. Cook 1 minute, stirring occasionally. Increase heat to high. Add mustard mixture to wok, stirring until slightly thickened and chicken is cooked through. Season to taste with salt and black pepper. Serve over hot cooked rice. Makes 4 servings.

About 280 calories per serving.

How to Make Curried Chicken with Fruit

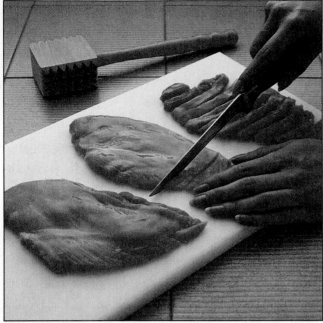

1/Using a cleaver or mallet, pound chicken until flattened; cut into 1/2-inch strips.

2/Add orange sections and kiwifruit slices; stir until heated through. Season to taste.

Curried Breast of Chicken with Fruit

Excellent flavor without too many calories.

1 lb. boneless chicken-breast halves, skinned
1 (8-oz.) can apricot halves in unsweetened juice
2/3 cup Chicken Broth, page 153, canned broth or water
1 tablespoon cornstarch
2 teaspoons peanut oil or vegetable oil

1 large onion, chopped
1 small tart apple, peeled, chopped
1 tablespoon curry powder
1 orange, peeled, sectioned
1 kiwifruit, peeled, sliced
Salt
Freshly ground black pepper

Using the flat side of a cleaver or meat mallet, pound chicken until flattened; cut into 1/2-inch strips. In a blender or food processor fitted with a metal blade, combine apricots with juice, 1/2 cup broth or water and cornstarch; process until smooth. Place wok over high heat; add oil. When hot, add chicken strips; stir-fry until firm and white through center. Remove from wok; set aside. Add onion and apple to wok; stir-fry 30 seconds. Sprinkle with remaining 2 to 3 tablespoons broth or water; stir-fry, covering wok occasionally to steam, until crisp-tender. Stir in curry powder. Pour apricot mixture over apple mixture; stir in cooked chicken. Cook, stirring until thickened. Add orange and kiwifruit; stir until heated through. Season to taste with salt and pepper. Makes 4 servings.

About 270 calories per serving.

Chicken with Fruit Sauce

This quick-cooking, delicious sauce will surprise and delight you.

1 lb. chicken thighs, boned, skinned
2 zucchini
2 yellow summer squash
2 teaspoons peanut oil or vegetable oil
1 garlic clove, crushed
1 onion, chopped

1 cup shredded bok choy or green cabbage
1 small, tart crisp apple, peeled, diced
4 small radishes, thinly sliced
1/4 cup thinly sliced green onions
2 cups hot cooked rice

Apricot-Apple Sauce:
1/4 cup apricot instant baby food
1/4 cup apple instant baby food
  or applesauce
1/2 cup Chicken Broth, page 153,
  canned broth or water

About 1/2 teaspoon curry powder
1/4 teaspoon salt

For sauce, in a food processor fitted with a metal blade, combine baby foods or applesauce, broth or water, curry powder and salt; process to a thick, smooth sauce.

For chicken, using the flat side of a cleaver or meat mallet, pound thighs to flatten slightly; cut into bite-sized pieces. Cut zucchini into thin matchsticks. Cut off narrow rounded tops from summer squash; save pieces for other use. Cut remaining squash into bite-sized cubes. Place wok over high heat; add oil. When hot, add garlic; stir-fry until lightly browned. Remove and discard garlic. Add chicken pieces to wok; stir-fry 1 minute. Add onion, zucchini and summer squash; stir-fry 3 minutes or until chicken is cooked through and vegetables are crisp-tender. Stir in bok choy or cabbage and apple; stir-fry 30 seconds.

To complete, add sauce to wok. Stir until hot and bubbly. Stir in radishes and green onions. Serve over hot cooked rice. Makes 4 servings.

Variation

Prepare this flavorful low-calorie sauce with other instant baby foods, same amount of broth or water and seasonings of your choice.

About 320 calories per serving.

How to Make Soy-Glazed Chicken

1/Lightly brown chicken breasts in hot wok; slowly add broth.

2/In a small bowl, combine carrot, onion and bok choy. Serve chicken over raw-vegetable mixture.

Soy-Glazed Chicken

Serve this Oriental-style chicken with steamed new potatoes and green beans.

2 boneless chicken-breast halves, skinned
Salt
1/4 cup Chicken Broth or Vegetable Broth,
   pages 152-153, canned broth or water
1 teaspoon sesame oil
2 tablespoons soy sauce
1 tablespoon dry sherry

1 tablespoon water
1 teaspoon honey
1 carrot, shredded
1 Vidalia onion or other sweet onion,
   chopped
1 cup shredded bok choy

Using the flat side of a cleaver or meat mallet, pound chicken until 1/4 inch thick; blot dry with paper towels. Place wok over high heat; sprinkle lightly with salt. When hot, salt will darken slightly. Add chicken pieces, not touching; cook 1 minute or until lightly browned. Turn and cook other side. Add broth or water; cover and steam 1 minute. Uncover and continue cooking, turning occasionally, until liquid has evaporated and chicken is firm and white through center. Remove from wok; set aside. Wipe wok clean with paper towels; place over medium-low heat. Add sesame oil, soy sauce, sherry, water and honey; stir to blend. Simmer 1 minute or until thick and syrupy. Return chicken to sauce; heat until hot through. In a small bowl, combine carrot, onion and bok choy. Serve chicken over raw-vegetable mixture. Makes 2 servings.

About 240 calories per serving.

Chicken with Plum Sauce

Oriental plum sauce makes this recipe special.

1 lb. chicken thighs, boned, skinned
1 tablespoon soy sauce
1 tablespoon dry sherry
2 teaspoons peanut oil or vegetable oil
1 large onion, chopped
1 garlic clove, minced

1/2 teaspoon minced gingerroot
1 large green bell pepper,
 cut in thin strips
1/2 cup water
1 tablespoon Oriental plum sauce
2 cups hot cooked rice

Using the flat side of a cleaver or meat mallet, pound chicken until flattened; cut lengthwise into narrow strips. In a small bowl, stir together soy sauce and sherry; stir in chicken strips until well coated. Cover and let stand 15 minutes. Place wok over high heat; add oil. When hot, add onion; stir-fry 1 minute or until crisp-tender. Stir in garlic, gingerroot and bell pepper; stir-fry 2 minutes or until pepper strips are crisp-tender. Push vegetables to 1 side of wok. Drain chicken, reserving marinade; add chicken to wok. Stir-fry chicken 2 minutes or until cooked through. Add water, reserved marinade and plum sauce; stir-fry until slightly thickened. Serve over hot cooked rice. Makes 4 servings.

About 290 calories per serving.

Chicken Véronique

A translation of a famous French recipe cooked in a wok.

1 lb. boneless chicken-breast halves,
 skinned
2 tablespoons dry white wine
1/4 Chicken Broth, page 153,
 canned broth or water
6 to 8 shallots, chopped
1/4 lb. mushrooms, chopped

1/4 teaspoon dried leaf tarragon
Salt
Freshly ground black pepper
1 teaspoon currant jelly
2 teaspoons Dijon-style mustard
1/2 cup seedless green grapes
2 cups hot cooked rice

Using the flat side of a cleaver or meat mallet, pound chicken until flattened; cut into 1/4-inch strips. Place wok over medium-high heat; add wine, broth or water, shallots and mushrooms. Simmer 1 minute. Add chicken; cook until firm and white through center. Stir in tarragon, salt, pepper, jelly and mustard. Cook, stirring constantly, until jelly melts and sauce is slightly thickened. Stir in grapes until heated through. Serve over hot cooked rice. Makes 4 servings.

About 290 calories per serving.

Salisbury Steak with Cumberland Sauce

An adaptation of a burger recipe from James Beard.

Cumberland Sauce:
1 teaspoon peanut oil or vegetable oil
1 garlic clove, minced
2 shallots, chopped
1/2 cup Chicken Broth, page 153,
  canned broth or water

1 teaspoon cornstarch
1/2 cup Madeira
2 teaspoons currant jelly

Meat Patties:
1 lb. ground raw turkey, thawed if frozen
1 tablespoon grated onion
1/2 teaspoon salt
1/4 teaspoon freshly ground black pepper

2 tablespoons evaporated skim milk
2 teaspoons peanut oil or vegetable oil
1/2 cup dry white wine or
  sparkling white wine

For sauce, heat oil in a small saucepan over low heat. When hot, add garlic and shallots; cook, stirring frequently, until softened. Add broth or water; simmer 5 minutes. Strain mixture through a fine sieve into top half of a double boiler. Stir cornstarch into Madeira. When smooth, add to garlic mixture. Add jelly; cook until thickened to a smooth sauce. Keep warm over simmering water until ready to serve.

For meat patties, in a large bowl, combine turkey, onion, salt, pepper and milk. Shape mixture into 4 patties. Place wok over high heat; add oil. When hot, add meat patties; cook 2 minutes, turning once on each side until browned. Reduce heat; add wine. Cover and steam 1 minute. Uncover and simmer in wine, turning patties once, until wine has almost entirely evaporated and meat has cooked through center. Serve patties with sauce. Makes 4 servings.

About 240 calories per serving.

Turkey Chorizo Patties

A hot, spicy turkey sausage, made in a Latin American style.

1 lb. ground raw turkey, thawed if frozen
1/2 tablespoon imported Hungarian
  hot paprika
1 teaspoon dried red-pepper flakes, crushed
1/2 teaspoon dried leaf oregano, crushed

1/4 teaspoon rubbed sage
3 tablespoons red-wine vinegar
3 tablespoons brandy
About 1 tablespoon peanut oil or
  vegetable oil

In a large bowl, combine turkey, paprika, red-pepper flakes, oregano and sage; blend well. Blend in vinegar and brandy. Cover and refrigerate 2 to 3 hours. Shape into 8 small patties. Place wok over high heat; coat bottom lightly with oil. When hot, fry 3 to 4 patties at a time until cooked through. Makes 8 patties or 4 servings.

About 200 calories per serving.

Dody's Special Stir-Fry

Great tasting and quick to prepare.

2 tablespoons grated Parmesan cheese
3 tablespoons Chicken Broth or
   Vegetable Broth, pages 152-153,
   canned broth or water
1 egg, lightly beaten
1 teaspoon peanut oil or vegetable oil
1/4 lb. mushrooms, sliced
1 small onion, chopped
1 garlic clove, minced

1 lb. ground raw turkey, thawed if frozen
1 teaspoon salt
1 teaspoon Italian Seasoning, page 155
1/4 cup dry red wine
2 to 3 dashes hot-pepper sauce
1 (10-oz.) pkg. frozen spinach or
   1 bunch fresh spinach, stems removed
2 cups hot cooked rice
6 cherry tomatoes, halved

In a small bowl, combine cheese, 1 tablespoon broth or water and egg; set aside. Using 1 teaspoon oil, lightly oil wok; place over high heat. When hot, add mushrooms and onion; stir-fry 1 minute. Sprinkle with remaining 2 tablespoons broth or water; cover and steam 1 minute. Uncover and increase heat to high. Stir in garlic and turkey; stir-fry, breaking up meat as it cooks, until no longer pink. Add salt, Italian Seasoning, wine and hot-pepper sauce; cover and steam 30 seconds. Uncover; stir-fry until liquid evaporates. Place spinach over turkey mixture; cover and steam 15 seconds or until slightly wilted. Stir spinach down into turkey mixture. Pour in cheese mixture; stir-fry until blended and dry. Serve over hot cooked rice. Garnish with cherry-tomato halves. Makes 4 servings.

About 330 calories per serving.

Mediterranean Turkey

A delicious way to enjoy low-calorie turkey.

2 teaspoons peanut oil or vegetable oil
3/4 lb. raw turkey dark meat,
   cut in thin strips
1 onion, diced
1 green bell pepper, diced
1 cucumber, seeded, diced
2 large tomatoes, chopped

1 teaspoon Italian Seasoning, page 155
1 tablespoon olive oil
2 tablespoons fresh lemon juice
Salt
Freshly ground black pepper
1/4 cup diced ripe olives
2 cups hot cooked rice

Place wok over high heat; add oil. When hot, add turkey; stir-fry 2 minutes or until nearly cooked through. Stir in onion, bell pepper and cucumber; stir-fry 1 minute. Add tomatoes, Italian Seasoning, olive oil and lemon juice. Season to taste with salt and black pepper. Stir in olives; stir-fry until heated through. Serve over hot cooked rice. Makes 4 servings.

About 310 calories per serving.

Indian Keema with Peas

Quick to prepare and hearty enough to satisfy any appetite.

2 teaspoons peanut oil or vegetable oil
1 small red onion, chopped
1 small garlic clove, minced
1 tablespoon curry powder
1/4 teaspoon ground cumin
1/4 ground coriander
1 lb. ground raw turkey, thawed if frozen
1 (16-oz.) can stewed tomatoes
1 tablespoon lime juice

2 tablespoons mango chutney,
  large pieces chopped
1/4 teaspoon dried red-pepper flakes,
  crushed
Salt
Freshly ground black pepper
1 cup fresh or thawed frozen green peas
2 cups hot cooked rice

Place wok over high heat; add oil. When hot, add onion; stir-fry 1 minute. Add garlic; stir-fry 30 seconds. Sprinkle with curry powder, cumin and coriander; stir-fry 30 seconds. Add ground turkey; stir-fry until no longer pink. Add tomatoes with juice, lime juice, chutney and red-pepper flakes. Season to taste with salt and black pepper. Bring to a boil. Reduce heat and cover; simmer 10 minutes. Stir in peas; cover and simmer 3 minutes or until peas are heated through. Serve over hot cooked rice. Makes 4 servings.

About 340 calories per serving.

Turkey Chili Con Carne

Here's another variation of this classic meal-in-a-bowl.

1 tablespoon peanut oil or vegetable oil
1 lb. raw turkey dark meat, chopped
1 onion, chopped
1 garlic clove, minced
About 1 tablespoon pure chili powder
1/2 teaspoon ground cumin
1/2 teaspoon ground coriander
1/2 teaspoon ground oregano
1 (28-oz.) can Italian-style peeled
  plum tomatoes

2 cups Vegetable Broth or Chicken Broth,
  pages 152-153, canned broth or water
Salt
1 tablespoon instant masa or white corn meal
Freshly ground black pepper
2 cups hot cooked rice
1 small lime, cut in wedges

Place wok over high heat; add oil. When hot, add turkey; stir-fry 1 minute. Add onion; stir-fry until softened. Stir in garlic, chili powder, cumin, coriander and oregano. Crush tomatoes; add to wok with juice and broth or water. Season with 1/2 teaspoon salt. Reduce heat and simmer 20 minutes. Stir in masa or corn meal; simmer 10 to 15 minutes, stirring frequently. Season to taste with salt and pepper. Serve over hot cooked rice with lime wedges. Makes 4 servings.

About 350 calories per serving.

Sicilian Stir-Fry with Turkey

A virtual Italian opera of flavors.

3 teaspoons peanut oil or vegetable oil
1 lb. raw turkey-breast slices,
  cut in thin strips
1 onion, diced
1 green bell pepper, diced
1 cucumber, peeled, diced
2 large tomatoes, chopped

2 teaspoons Italian Seasoning, page 155
2 teaspoons olive oil
1 tablespoon fresh lemon juice
Salt
Freshly ground black pepper
1/4 cup diced ripe olives
2 cups hot cooked rice

Place wok over high heat; add 2 teaspoons peanut oil or vegetable oil. When hot, add turkey; stir-fry 4 to 5 minutes or until meat starts to brown. Remove from wok; set aside. Reduce heat to medium; add remaining 1 teaspoon peanut oil or vegetable oil. Add onion and bell pepper; stir-fry 1 minute. Add cucumber and tomatoes; stir-fry 1 minute. Cover and steam until vegetables give off some liquid. Stir in Italian Seasoning, olive oil and lemon juice. Season to taste with salt and black pepper. Return browned turkey strips to wok; stir-fry 1 minute. Cover and steam 1 minute or until turkey is cooked through. Stir in olives. Serve over hot cooked rice. Makes 4 servings.

About 340 calories per serving.

Near-East Turkey Stir-Fry

Turkey is a delicious source of protein and very low in fat.

1 large onion, chopped
2 tablespoons water
1/4 cup soy sauce
1/4 cup dry sherry
1 garlic clove, minced
1 (1-inch) piece gingerroot, minced

1 lb. ground raw turkey, thawed if frozen
4 oz. Chinese or Italian vermicelli
1 (6-oz.) pkg. frozen edible pea pods
6 to 8 canned water chestnuts,
  coarsely chopped

Place wok over high heat. When hot, add onion; stir-fry 1 minute. Sprinkle with water; cover and steam 30 seconds. Remove from heat; add soy sauce, sherry, garlic and gingerroot. Stir in turkey; let stand 15 minutes. Place Chinese vermicelli in a large bowl; cover with boiling water. Let stand 15 minutes. Or, cook Italian vermicelli according to package directions until tender but firm to the bite; drain cooked pasta. Return wok to medium heat. Stir-fry 5 minutes or until turkey is no longer pink. Add pea pods and water chestnuts; stir until pea pods and water chestnuts are heated through. Stir in cooked pasta; toss to mix. Serve immediately. Makes 4 servings.

About 310 calories per serving.

Huevos Rancheros

An all-time favorite from south of the border.

4 large crisp lettuce leaves
About 3 teaspoons peanut oil or
   vegetable oil
4 (6-inch) corn tortillas or
   flour tortillas
1 small onion, chopped
1/2 small green bell pepper, chopped
1/4 cup canned diced green chilies, drained
1 large tomato, chopped

3 eggs
2 egg whites
1/8 teaspoon salt
1/8 teaspoon freshly ground black pepper
2 or 3 dashes hot-pepper sauce
1/2 cup shredded Monterey Jack
   cheese (2 oz.)
Chili powder, if desired

Arrange lettuce leaves on 4 small plates. Using 1/2 teaspoon oil, lightly oil bottom and side of wok. Place wok over high heat. When hot, add tortillas, 1 at a time, cooking until lightly browned on both sides. Oil wok as needed. Place each hot tortilla over lettuce. Place 1 teaspoon oil in wok. When hot, add onion and bell pepper; stir-fry over high heat until crisp-tender. Add green chilies and tomato; stir-fry until heated through. Spoon over hot tortillas, dividing mixture evenly. In a medium bowl, beat together eggs and egg whites until well blended. Add salt, black pepper and hot-pepper sauce. Add remaining 1 teaspoon oil to wok. When hot, add egg mixture; stir until slightly scrambled. Spoon over hot tortillas. Sprinkle each egg mound with cheese. Add a dash of chili powder to each, if desired. Garnish as desired. Makes 4 servings.

About 200 calories per serving.

Chili Omelet with Rice

Easy and great tasting; the perfect recipe for when you're too tired to cook.

4 eggs
2 egg whites
1/2 cup cold cooked rice
1 teaspoon pure chili powder
1/2 teaspoon salt

1/8 teaspoon freshly ground black pepper
1/4 cup chopped onion
1/2 green bell pepper, chopped
1 tablespoon butter

In a medium bowl, beat eggs and egg whites until blended; stir in rice, chili powder, salt and black pepper. Place wok over high heat. When hot, add onion and bell pepper; stir-fry 1 minute or until crisp-tender. Reduce heat to medium-low; add butter. When melted, pour in egg mixture; cook until set on bottom and sides. Gently lift cooked portion with spatula so that uncooked portion can flow to bottom. Cook until top is firm. Fold over and turn out onto warm plates. Makes 2 servings.

About 270 calories per serving.

Huevos Rancheros

Eggs with Tomato Sauce

Perfect for that light, festive luncheon.

3 Swedish-style bran fiber bread crackers
4 eggs
2 egg whites
2 tablespoons evaporated skim milk
1/2 teaspoon Italian Seasoning, page 155
1/2 teaspoon salt

1/8 teaspoon freshly ground black pepper
1 tablespoon peanut oil or vegetable oil
2 cups Fresh Tomato Sauce or
   Quick Tomato Sauce, page 154
1 tablespoon grated Parmesan cheese

In a blender or food processor fitted with a metal blade, process crackers to coarse crumbs. In a medium bowl, beat together eggs and egg whites. Blend in cracker crumbs, milk, Italian Seasoning, salt and pepper. Lightly oil wok; place over medium heat. When hot, spoon in about 2 tablespoons egg mixture. Cook until lightly browned; then turn and brown other side. Transfer to a cooling rack. Repeat using remaining batter, oiling wok as needed, until all egg is prepared. Roll each cooked omelet; cut into narrow strips. Pour tomato sauce into wok; bring to a simmer over medium heat. Add omelet strips; stir gently until reheated. Serve on individual plates, sprinkled with Parmesan cheese. Makes 4 servings.

About 190 calories per serving.

Egg Fu Yung with Langostinos

Langostinos taste like shrimp and crab, but cost much less.

6 to 8 crisp curly lettuce leaves
3 eggs
1 egg white
1 cup fresh or frozen green peas
4 water chestnuts, coarsely chopped
1 teaspoon soy sauce

1 (6-oz.) pkg. frozen langostinos
   or shrimp, cooked
2 teaspoons peanut oil or vegetable oil
1 tablespoon chopped green onion
Cherry-tomato halves
Parsley sprigs

Arrange lettuce leaves on 2 small plates to form cups. Place frozen langostinos in a colander; set over a bowl 30 minutes or until thawed and drained. Wrap thawed langostinos in a clean towel; squeeze out all liquid. In a medium bowl, combine eggs and egg white until blended; stir in peas, water chestnuts, soy sauce and langostinos or shrimp. Place wok over medium heat; add oil. When hot, pour in egg mixture; stir until lightly scrambled but still moist. Spoon cooked egg into lettuce cups, dividing evenly. Sprinkle with green onion. Garnish with cherry-tomato halves and parsley. Makes 2 servings.

About 320 calories per serving.

How to Make Custard with Spinach & Shrimp

1/Arrange 1 shrimp in each custard cup with tail extending over rim. Place spinach, mushrooms and carrot in each cup.

2/Place cups on a rack over simmering water. Add egg mixture to each custard cup.

Steamed Custard with Spinach & Shrimp

The perfect low-calorie choice for breakfast or brunch.

4 large cooked shrimp, unpeeled
4 large spinach leaves, shredded
2 large mushrooms, sliced
4 thin cooked-carrot slices
2 eggs

1 cup Japanese-Style Stock, page 151;
  Chicken Broth, page 153;
  canned broth or water
1 teaspoon soy sauce

Peel and devein shrimp, leaving last segment of shell and tail attached. Arrange 1 shrimp in each of 4 (1- to 1-1/2-cup) custard cups with tail extending over rim of cups. Place 1/4 of spinach in the bottom of each cup. Add 1/4 of mushrooms and 1 carrot slice to each cup. In a medium bowl, beat eggs until frothy. Stir in broth or water and soy sauce. Place cups on a rack in a wok over simmering water; pour egg mixture into each cup, dividing evenly. Cover and steam 10 to 12 minutes or until slightly firm. Makes 4 servings.

About 80 calories per serving.

Shirred Eggs with Ham & Peaches

A truly beautiful luncheon dish or light dinner entree.

8 to 12 thin asparagus spears
2 thin lean cooked ham slices
1 teaspoon Dijon-style mustard
2 peaches
1 teaspoon fresh lemon juice
2 teaspoons sugar
2 or 3 drops peanut oil or vegetable oil
1 teaspoon minced chives
1 teaspoon minced parsley

2 eggs
Salt
Freshly ground black pepper
1 tablespoon dry white wine
1 tablespoon evaporated skim milk
2 thin slices whole-wheat bread, toasted,
  cut in rounds
Parsley sprigs

Break tough ends from asparagus; rinse under cold running water. Place asparagus in a single layer on a rack in a wok over simmering water. Cover and steam 6 to 8 minutes or until crisp-tender; remove from wok. Spread each ham slice lightly with mustard; top each with 1/2 of asparagus. Roll ham, enclosing asparagus; secure with cocktail picks. Bring a small pan of water to a boil. Plunge each peach into boiling water 30 seconds; then hold under cold running water and slip off skin. Cut each peach in 1/2, removing pits. Sprinkle cut halves with lemon juice and sugar; set aside. Lightly oil 2 (1-cup) custard cups. Combine chives and parsley; sprinkle in custard cups, dividing evenly. Break an egg into each cup; sprinkle with salt and pepper. In a small bowl, combine wine and milk; pour 1/2 of mixture over each egg. Place custard cups in center of a shallow steaming dish. Add ham bundles and peach halves on either side. Place dish on a rack in a wok over simmering water. Cover and steam 8 to 10 minutes or until eggs are firm. Remove steaming dish from wok. Place 1 toasted bread round on each serving plate. Invert 1 egg onto each bread round. Arrange a ham bundle and 2 peach halves on either side of each egg. Garnish each plate with parsley. Makes 2 servings.

About 220 calories per serving.

Shirred Eggs with Tomatoes & Mustard

Shirred eggs should be served immediately because they continue to cook while standing.

1 small tomato
4 teaspoons evaporated skim milk
1 teaspoon Dijon-style mustard

4 eggs
Salt
Freshly ground black pepper

Cut tomato in 1/2; squeeze out and discard seeds and juice. Cut tomato halves into thin strips. Pat dry with paper towels; then finely dice. In a small bowl, stir together milk and mustard. Lightly oil 4 (1-cup) ramekin or custard cups; break 1 egg into each cup. Sprinkle each with diced tomato. Divide milk mixture between cups. Place cups in a shallow steaming dish; place dish on a rack in a wok over simmering water. Cover and steam 6 to 8 minutes or until whites have set and yolks are slightly firm. Sprinkle evenly with salt and pepper. Serve immediately. Makes 4 servings.

About 90 calories per serving.

FISH & SHELLFISH

Fish and shellfish are more popular today than ever before. They have become a standard entree, low in calories yet tasty and quick to prepare. And best of all, people are enjoying fish and shellfish blended with herbs, vegetables and other flavorful ingredients.

No matter what type of fish you buy, freshness counts most. Although quality fresh fish is difficult to find in some areas, the frozen fish case offers a variety of choices that can be included in diet meals.

Many diets recommend eating only plain broiled fish. This may become tiring and rather mundane. Recipes in this chapter will show you how fish can be moist, mouth-watering and still low in calories. And best of all, fish can be cooked quickly in your wok over high heat to minimize moisture lose. For a new flavor, add your favorite sauce or wine when cooking fish. Stir-fry fish to serve with a fresh tomato sauce. Or, steam packets of foil-wrapped fish with well-seasoned liquid. Fish can be wok-cooked in many completely different ways, but not one will give you dry and tasteless fish—that's a promise!

Menu

Breakfast
2 pieces whole-wheat toast
1 oz. low-fat ricotta cheese
2 teaspoons low-calorie jelly
1/2 grapefruit
Coffee or tea

Snack
Coffee or tea   3 crackers

Lunch
Tossed green salad with 1 tablespoon low-calorie dressing
2 flatbread crackers

Dinner
Linguine with Mushroom Sauce, page 125
6 oz. white wine
Filet of Sole with Rice & Bean Sprouts, page 85
1 croissant   1 oz. cream cheese
Coffee or tea

About 1200 calories

Quick & Delicious Seafood Chowder

A basic chowder you will make again and again.

2 large tomatoes, peeled
2 teaspoons peanut oil or vegetable oil
1 carrot, finely diced
1 celery stalk, diced
1 Vidalia onion or other sweet onion,
  thinly sliced
1 small green bell pepper, diced
1/2 teaspoon dried leaf tarragon
1/2 teaspoon dried leaf thyme
1/4 teaspoon dried red-pepper flakes

1/2 cup bottled clam juice
1 cup water
1/4 cup dry white wine or vermouth
1/2 lb. boiling potatoes, peeled, diced
1/2 teaspoon salt
1 (6-oz.) pkg. thawed frozen langostinos
  or shrimp
1 (1-lb.) pkg. thawed frozen cod or
  flounder fillets
1 tablespoon minced parsley

Cut tomatoes into chunks, reserving juice. Place wok over medium-high heat; add oil. When hot, add carrot, celery, onion and bell pepper; stir-fry 1 minute. Add tomatoes with juice, tarragon, thyme and red-pepper flakes; stir-fry 1 minute. Add clam juice, water and wine or vermouth; stir to blend. Place potatoes on top of vegetables; sprinkle with 1/4 teaspoon salt. Bring to a boil; reduce heat. Cover and simmer 10 minutes or until potatoes are tender. Place langostinos or shrimp and fish fillets in a single layer over potatoes; sprinkle with remaining salt. Cover and simmer 3 to 4 minutes or until fish is opaque and flakes easily with a fork. Using a fork, break fish fillets into chunks. Stir fish and langostinos or shrimp down into chowder. Ladle into large shallow soup bowls. Sprinkle each serving with minced parsley. Makes 4 servings.

About 240 calories per serving.

Stir-Fried Crabmeat with Mushrooms

Crabmeat may be costly, but is well worth the price for this special dish.

2 teaspoons peanut oil or vegetable oil
1/2 lb. mushrooms, coarsely chopped
1/2 cup chopped green onions
16 cherry tomatoes, halved
1/2 lb. fresh or thawed frozen crabmeat,
  drained, flaked

3 tablespoons Oloroso or
  other medium-sweet sherry
1 tablespoon fresh lemon juice
1 cup hot cooked rice
Minced fresh parsley
Lemon wedges

Place wok over high heat; add oil. When hot, add mushrooms and green onions; stir-fry 1 minute. Add tomatoes, crabmeat, sherry and lemon juice; stir-fry until heated through. Spoon over hot cooked rice. Garnish with parsley and lemon wedges. Makes 2 servings.

About 320 calories per serving.

Shrimp with Tomatoes & Hot Peppers

A great dish if you like your shrimp slightly hot with pepper.

2 teaspoons peanut oil or vegetable oil
1 small onion, chopped
1 small garlic clove, minced
1/8 teaspoon dried red-pepper flakes or
   1 small dried hot red pepper,
   seeded, crushed

1 (12-oz.) can Italian-style
   peeled plum tomatoes
1-1/2 lbs. medium shrimp, peeled, deveined
Salt
Freshly ground black pepper
2 cups hot cooked rice

Place wok over high heat; add oil. When hot, add onion and garlic; stir-fry until tender. Stir in red pepper and tomatoes with juice; boil, stirring to break up tomatoes, until reduced by 1/2. Add shrimp; cook, stirring constantly, until pink. Season to taste with salt and black pepper. Serve over hot cooked rice. Makes 4 servings.

About 310 calories per serving.

Pork & Scallop Stir-Fry

Meat and seafood are combined with superb results in this Chinese-style dish.

1 lb. scallops, halved if large
1 tablespoon sherry
1 tablespoon cornstarch
1/4 teaspoon white pepper
1/4 teaspoon salt
2 teaspoons peanut oil or vegetable oil
1 garlic clove, crushed
3 oz. Chinese Red-Braised Pork, drained,
   slivered, page 46

2 small cucumbers, peeled, seeded,
   cut in 1/2-inch cubes
1 (10-oz.) pkg. frozen edible pea pods
2 tablespoons marinade from
   Chinese Red-Braised Pork, page 46
2 cups hot cooked rice
2 tablespoons chopped green onion

In a medium bowl, combine scallops, sherry, cornstarch, white pepper and salt; toss to coat. Let stand 30 minutes. Place wok over high heat; add oil. When hot, add garlic; stir-fry until browned. Remove and discard garlic. Drain and add scallops; stir-fry 30 seconds. Add pork, cucumbers, pea pods and marinade from pork; stir-fry 1 minute. Serve over hot cooked rice. Garnish with green onion. Makes 4 servings.

About 310 calories per serving.

Scampi

Large shrimp cooked to perfection in garlic and white wine.

8 dried shiitake mushrooms
1/4 cup water
1 tablespoon dry sherry or white wine
1/4 cup clam juice or water
2 thin lemon slices
1 teaspoon peanut oil or vegetable oil
1 small onion, chopped
1 large garlic clove, slivered

2 teaspoons olive oil or other mild,
    fruity tasting oil
16 large shrimp, peeled, deveined
10 oz. fresh or frozen edible pea pods
About 2 teaspoons fresh lemon juice
Soy sauce or salt
2 cups hot cooked rice

In a small saucepan, combine mushrooms, water and sherry or wine; bring to a simmer. Cover and let stand over low heat 10 minutes; do not boil. Remove from heat. Remove and discard mushroom stems; blot mushroom caps dry. Cut caps in quarters. Stir clam juice or water into mushroom liquid. Cut each lemon slice into 4 wedges. Place wok over high heat; add peanut oil or vegetable oil. When hot, add onion and garlic; stir-fry until tender but not browned. Add lemon wedges and olive oil; when hot, add shrimp and mushroom caps. Stir-fry about 1 minute. Pour in mushroom liquid; bring to a boil, stirring ingredients until shrimp are pink. Stir in pea pods; cover and steam 1 minute. Season to taste with lemon juice and soy sauce or salt. Serve with hot cooked rice. Makes 4 servings.

About 210 calories per serving.

Stir-Fried Shrimp with Endive

Colorful pink shrimp are a perfect contrast to creamy white endive.

1 tablespoon dry sherry
2 tablespoons soy sauce
3/4 teaspoon sugar
1/4 cup water
1 teaspoon cornstarch
2 teaspoons peanut oil or vegetable oil
4 Belgian endive, cut crosswise
    in 1/4-inch slices

1/2 teaspoon salt
1 lb. medium shrimp, peeled, deveined
1 teaspoon minced garlic
1 teaspoon grated gingerroot
2 cups hot cooked rice

In a small bowl, combine sherry, soy sauce, 1/2 teaspoon sugar and water; stir in cornstarch until smooth. Place wok over high heat; add oil. When hot, add endive; stir-fry 1 minute. Sprinkle with remaining 1/4 teaspoon sugar and salt; stir-fry 30 seconds. Add shrimp; stir-fry until pink. Stir in garlic, gingerroot and cornstarch mixture; cook, stirring frequently, until mixture is slightly thickened. Serve over hot cooked rice. Makes 4 servings.

About 280 calories per serving.

Seafood Quenelles with Vegetables

A colorful and flavorful entree.

1/2 lb. medium shrimp, peeled, deveined
1/2 lb. haddock, flounder, sole or
  other white-fish fillets
1 teaspoon onion juice
1 teaspoon fresh ginger juice
1 tablespoon fresh lemon juice
2 egg whites
1 teaspoon salt
Freshly ground black pepper
6 oz. fresh or frozen edible pea pods

1 garlic clove, minced
1 (1-inch) piece gingerroot, minced
1/2 cup broccoli flowerets, chopped
1 cup coarsely chopped mushrooms
2 cups loosely packed shredded bok choy or
  Chinese cabbage
2 teaspoons peanut oil or vegetable oil
1 tablespoon water
2 cups hot cooked rice
2 green onions, minced

In a food processor fitted with a metal blade, combine shrimp and fish; process to a soft paste. Add onion juice, ginger juice and lemon juice; blend well. Add egg whites, 1 at a time, blending well after each addition. Season to taste with salt and pepper. Or, place shrimp and fish on a flat surface. Using a cleaver or sharp knife, chop into very fine pieces. Add other ingredients as above. Shape mixture into egg-shaped balls. Fill a wok about 1/2 full with water; bring to a simmer over medium-high heat. Add fish balls, a few at a time; cook, turning gently until firm, about 1 minute. Remove with a slotted spoon; set aside. If desired, cooked fish balls may be refrigerated several hours before using. In a medium bowl, combine pea pods, garlic, gingerroot, broccoli, mushrooms and bok choy or Chinese cabbage. Place wok over high heat; add oil. When hot, add vegetable mixture; stir-fry 1 to 2 minutes. Sprinkle with water; cover and steam 1 minute. Continue to stir-fry until vegetables are crisp-tender. Add prepared fish balls; gently stir into vegetables. Continue to stir-fry, lifting fish balls carefully so they do not fall apart. When mixture is heated through, serve over hot cooked rice. Sprinkle with green onions. Makes 4 servings.

About 270 calories per serving.

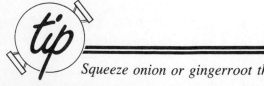

Squeeze onion or gingerroot through a garlic press to make fresh juice.

How to Make Seafood Quenelles with Vegetables

1/Shape seafood mixture into egg-shaped balls. Add quenelles to simmering water. Cook, a few at a time, until firm. Remove with a slotted spoon.

2/Add prepared seafood quenelles to vegetable mixture. Continue to stir-fry, lifting quenelles carefully so they do not fall apart. When heated through, serve over rice.

Dalmatian Fish Stew

A Southern dish traditionally served for a hunt-club breakfast buffet.

2 teaspoons peanut oil or vegetable oil
2 onions, thinly sliced
1 (12-oz.) pkg. individually frozen fish
   fillets, thawed
1/2 teaspoon dried leaf basil
Water

2 tablespoons tomato paste or ketchup
1/2 cup dry white wine
Salt
Freshly ground black pepper
2 cups hot cooked rice
Minced fresh parsley

Place wok over medium heat; add oil. When hot, add 1/2 onion slices; stir-fry 1 minute. Arrange fish fillets in a single layer over onion slices. Season with basil; place remaining onion slices over top. Sprinkle with 2 tablespoons water; cover and steam 3 to 4 minutes or until onions are transparent and fish is opaque and flakes easily with a fork. In a small bowl, combine tomato paste or ketchup, 1/2 cup water and wine; pour over onions and fish. Remove from heat; cover and steam 1 minute. Season to taste with salt and pepper. Serve over hot cooked rice. Garnish with parsley. Makes 3 servings.

About 300 calories per serving.

Elsie's Fillet of Fish

My friend Elsie Pearce developed this great-tasting recipe while she was dieting.

Salt
1 (12-oz.) pkg. individually frozen fish
   fillets, such as flounder, perch,
   haddock or cod, thawed
1/2 teaspoon herbs of Provence
1/4 small green bell pepper,
   cut in thin strips

1/2 small onion, thinly sliced
3 tablespoons Vegetable Broth,
   page 152, or water
Fresh lemon juice
Freshly ground black pepper

Place wok over high heat; sprinkle lightly with salt. When hot, salt will darken slightly. Add fish fillets in a single layer. Sprinkle with herbs and 1/4 teaspoon salt; top with bell pepper and onion. When lightly browned, turn each fillet with a spatula. Pour in broth or water; cover and steam 1 minute. Uncover and cook until fish is opaque and flakes easily with a fork. Transfer fish to serving plates. Spoon cooking liquid over fish. Sprinkle with lemon juice; season to taste with black pepper. Makes 3 servings.

About 100 calories per serving.

White Fish in Cream Sauce

Rich, creamy flavor without the extra calories of cream.

1 tablespoon low-fat ricotta cheese
1 tablespoon plain low-fat yogurt
Salt
1/8 teaspoon curry powder, if desired
2 thick haddock fillets or
   other white fish fillets, about 1/2 lb.

1 onion, thinly sliced
Freshly ground black pepper
Chopped fresh cilantro or parsley
1 small lemon, quartered

In a small bowl, combine cheese and yogurt; beat until smooth. Season with 1/8 teaspoon salt and curry powder, if desired. Spread mixture evenly on each fish fillet. Arrange fillets in a shallow dish; refrigerate 1 hour. Cut 2 (12-inch-square) foil pieces; place each fillet on a foil piece. Top each fillet with onion slices; sprinkle with pepper, cilantro or parsley, and salt, if desired. Bring sides of each foil piece up toward center; seal with a drug-store fold, leaving sufficient room for steaming, page 87. Place sealed fish packets on a rack in a wok over simmering water; cover and steam 8 to 10 minutes. Transfer packets to plates; slit open. Top each with 2 lemon wedges. Makes 2 servings.

About 120 calories per serving.

tip

Cilantro may also be known as fresh coriander, Chinese parsley or Mexican parsley.

How to Make Elsie's Fillet of Fish

1/Place wok over high heat; sprinkle with salt. When hot, salt will darken slightly. Add fish fillets in a single layer.

2/Sprinkle fish with herbs and salt. Top with onion slices and bell-pepper strips.

Sweet & Sour Sole

Easy on the cook and the budget.

1 tablespoon cornstarch
1 cup unsweetened pineapple juice
1/2 cup Vegetable Broth, page 152, or water
2 tablespoons white-wine vinegar
1 teaspoon sugar
About 1/4 teaspoon salt
1/4 cup dry sherry
1 teaspoon peanut oil or vegetable oil

1 small onion, cut in wedges, separated
1 small green bell pepper,
cut in 1-inch squares
1 (12-oz.) pkg. individually frozen sole
fillets, thawed
Freshly ground black pepper
2 cups hot cooked rice

In a small bowl, stir together cornstarch and pineapple juice until smooth; stir in broth or water, vinegar, sugar, 1/4 teaspoon salt and sherry; set aside. Lightly oil bottom and side of wok; place over high heat. When hot, add onion pieces and bell-pepper squares; stir-fry 1 minute. Stir cornstarch mixture into wok; reduce heat and simmer mixture 2 to 3 minutes or until it begins to thicken, stirring frequently. Arrange fish fillets in simmering sauce. Spoon a little sauce over surface of each fillet. Cover and cook 2 minutes. Remove wok from heat; cover and let stand 2 minutes or until fish is opaque and flakes easily with a fork. Season to taste with salt and black pepper. Serve over hot cooked rice. Makes 3 servings.

About 330 calories per serving.

Fish with Green Beans & Potatoes

A tangy mustard sauce gives this low-calorie steamed dinner a superb flavor.

1/2 lb. young green beans
4 small new potatoes
1 lb. fish fillets, such as sole,
   snapper, halibut or flounder
4 to 6 large spinach or romaine leaves
2 tomatoes, cut in wedges
1 lime
1 tablespoon Dijon-style mustard
2 tablespoons vegetable oil

1/2 cup plain low-fat yogurt
1/2 teaspoon dried leaf tarragon
1 tablespoon minced watercress,
   spinach or parsley
1 teaspoon sugar
Salt
Freshly ground black pepper
2 tablespoons sliced ripe olives

Place green beans in a steamer dish on a rack in a wok over simmering water; cover and steam 6 to 8 minutes or until crisp-tender. Remove and set aside. Add additional water to wok, if necessary. Place unpeeled potatoes on a rack in wok over simmering water; cover and steam until easily pierced. Remove and set aside. Check water in wok; add water for steaming, if necessary. Arrange fish fillets in steaming dish over simmering water; cover and steam until fish is opaque and flakes easily with a fork. Cover a large platter with spinach or romaine leaves; arrange fish in center of platter. Surround with steamed green beans, potatoes and tomato wedges. Grate peel from lime; juice lime. Place mustard in a small bowl; gradually beat in oil with a whisk until blended. Add lime juice and peel; stir in yogurt, tarragon and watercress, spinach or parsley. Add sugar; season to taste with salt and pepper. To serve, pour sauce over fish and vegetables; sprinkle with olives. Makes 4 servings.

About 230 calories per serving.

Cod in Creole Sauce

Lots of flavor, but few calories.

1 small green bell pepper,
  cut in thin strips
1 small red bell pepper, cut in thin strips
1 small onion, chopped
1/2 cup thinly sliced celery
1 garlic clove, minced
2 tablespoons minced green onion
2 tablespoons Chicken Broth, page 153,
  canned broth or water
2 tablespoons dry white wine

1 (12-oz.) can stewed tomatoes
2 tablespoons tomato paste
1/8 teaspoon Italian Seasoning, page 155
1/8 teaspoon dried red-pepper flakes
1/4 teaspoon salt
1/8 teaspoon freshly ground black pepper
1 (12-oz.) pkg. individually frozen
  cod fillets, thawed
2 cups hot cooked rice
Minced fresh parsley

Place wok over high heat. When hot, add bell peppers, onion and celery; stir-fry 1 minute. Add garlic and green onion; stir-fry 30 seconds. Drizzle with broth or water; cover and steam 1 minute or until vegetables are crisp-tender. Add wine; boil 1 minute. Stir in tomatoes and tomato paste. Add Italian Seasoning, pepper flakes, salt and black pepper. Reduce heat and simmer 10 minutes or until thickened. Arrange fish fillets in a single layer over sauce; spoon a little sauce over each fillet. Simmer 5 minutes or until fish is opaque and flakes easily with a fork. Break fish into bite-sized pieces. Spoon fish and sauce over hot-cooked rice. Garnish with parsley. Makes 3 servings.

About 310 calories per serving.

Fillet of Sole with Rice & Bean Sprouts

Even if you're not dieting, you'll want to experience the great taste of this entree.

2 thick sole fillets, about 3/4 lb.
2 tablespoons lemon juice
2 tablespoons dry white wine or vermouth
2 tablespoons clam juice
2 tablespoons water

1 cup hot cooked rice
1 cup mung bean sprouts, rinsed,
  drained, blotted dry
Salt
Freshly ground black pepper

Pat sole fillets dry with paper towels. Place wok over high heat. When hot, add fillets in a single layer. Cook 1 minute; turn and cook other side 1 minute. Pour lemon juice, wine or vermouth, clam juice and water over fish; turn fish in liquid. Boil about 30 seconds. Remove wok from heat; cover and steep 1 minute or until fish is opaque and flakes easily with a fork. In a small bowl, combine rice and bean sprouts; arrange mixture on 2 serving plates. Remove fish from wok with a slotted spatula, draining slightly; place over rice on serving plates. Pour any liquid in wok over surface of fish. Season to taste with salt and black pepper. Makes 2 servings.

About 280 calories per serving.

Ginger-Steeped Fish Fillets & Noodles

Serve as part of an Oriental buffet or as a main-course entree.

1 (1-inch) piece gingerroot, crushed
1 small garlic clove, crushed
1/4 cup dry sherry
1/2 small lemon, unpeeled, chopped

1/4 teaspoon salt
4 thick sole fillets, about 1 lb.
1/4 teaspoon vegetable oil
5 to 6 oz. Chinese vermicelli

Hot-Pepper Sauce:
3/4 cup water
1 tablespoon red-wine vinegar
2 teaspoons light-brown sugar

3 tablespoons soy sauce
2 teaspoons cornstarch
2 small red hot chilies, seeded, chopped

For sauce, in a small saucepan, combine 1/2 cup water, vinegar, brown sugar and soy sauce; stir until sugar dissolves. In a small bowl, stir together cornstarch and remaining 1/4 cup water until smooth; stir into hot liquid, cooking until slightly thickened. Stir in chilies. Keep hot until ready to serve.

For fish, pour 4 cups water in a wok; place over medium heat. Add gingerroot, garlic, sherry, lemon and salt; bring to a full boil. Reduce heat and simmer 15 minutes. Place fish fillets in liquid; remove wok from heat. Cover and steep 5 to 6 minutes or until fish is opaque and flakes easily with a fork.

For pasta, in a large saucepan, bring 3 to 4 quarts water to a boil. Add 1/4 teaspoon oil and vermicelli; cook 2 minutes or until tender but firm to the bite.

To complete, drain cooked pasta; spread in a long shallow serving dish. Using a slotted spatula, remove fillets; place over cooked vermicelli. Top with Hot-Pepper Sauce. Makes 4 servings.

About 280 calories per serving.

How to Make Sole with Potatoes & Asparagus

1/Place ingredients on foil piece as directed in recipe. Bring sides of each foil piece up toward center.

2/Seal with a drug-store fold, leaving sufficient room for steaming. Place sealed packets on a rack in a wok.

Sole with Potatoes & Asparagus   *Photo on cover.*

An entree to celebrate the coming of Spring!

4 to 6 small new potatoes
12 thin asparagus spears
Salt, if desired
2 flounder or sole fillets
6 to 8 medium shrimp, peeled, deveined

About 1 teaspoon soy sauce
About 1 teaspoon lime juice
Freshly ground black pepper
Chopped fresh dill

Place unpeeled potatoes on a rack in a wok over simmering water; cover and steam until easily pierced. Cool slightly; cut potatoes into thick slices. Break tough ends from asparagus; rinse. Place asparagus in a single layer on a rack in a wok over simmering water; cover and steam 2 to 3 minutes. Remove and set aside. Add additional hot water to wok, if necessary. Cut 2 (12- to 14-inch-square) foil pieces. Place potato slices evenly on center of each foil square; season with salt, if desired. Top each packet with a fish fillet and 3 to 4 shrimp. Arrange 3 asparagus spears on each side of each fish fillet. Season with soy sauce, lime juice, pepper and dill. Bring sides of each foil piece up toward center; seal with a drug-store fold, leaving sufficient room for steaming. Place sealed packets on a rack in a wok over simmering water; cover and steam 8 to 10 minutes. Makes 2 servings.

Variation

Steam potatoes in a steamer basket until nearly tender. Add asparagus and fish to steamer. Top fish with shrimp. Season as desired. Cover and steam 4 to 6 minutes or until fish is opaque and flakes easily with a fork. Asparagus should be crisp-tender.

About 150 calories per serving.

Grand Aioli Platter

A great specialty of Provence, updated and served with fresh cod and garlic-flavored hollandaise.

12 small new potatoes
1/2 lb. carrots, cut in 2" x 1/4" strips
1/4 lb. young green beans, halved lengthwise
2 red or green bell peppers,
   cut in 1/2-inch strips

1 lb. cod fillets
About 1/4 cup fresh lemon juice
1 tablespoon minced green onion

Garlicky Hollandaise:
2 eggs, room temperature
1 tablespoon tarragon vinegar
1 tablespoon fresh lemon juice
2 tablespoons hot water
1 small garlic clove, minced

1 teaspoon Dijon-style mustard
Pinch red (cayenne) pepper
Salt
Freshly ground black pepper

Place unpeeled potatoes on a rack in a wok over simmmering water; cover and steam 10 to 15 minutes or until easily pierced. Remove from wok; place on a large platter. Place carrots and beans in a steaming dish on a rack in wok over simmering water; cover and steam 6 to 8 minutes or until crisp-tender. If necessary, add additional water to wok; add bell pepper to dish. Steam until vegetables are crisp-tender; arrange on a platter with steamed potatoes. Arrange fish fillets in steaming dish; sprinkle with lemon juice and green onion. Cover and steam 5 to 6 minutes or until fish is opaque and flakes easily with a fork. Transfer with a slotted spatula to platter. Cool fish and vegetables to room temperature.

For hollandaise, in a medium, heatproof bowl or top of a double boiler, combine eggs, vinegar, lemon juice and water; place over a saucepan of simmering water. Beat with a whisk until fluffy and thick. Remove bowl or pan from water. Add garlic, mustard and red pepper; beat until well blended. Season to taste with salt and black pepper. Make and refrigerate up to 3 hours ahead.

To complete, place bowl of hollandaise over hot water; whisk mixture 30 seconds to blend. Top each serving of fish and vegetables with a heaping tablespoon of hollandaise. Serve immediately. Makes 4 servings.

About 220 calories per serving.

This hollandaise sauce is excellent over any steamed vegetable, fish or chicken dish.

Sole & Shrimp Imperial

Incredibly easy; exceptionally good.

1 teaspoon cornstarch
1 teaspoon dry mustard
1/4 teaspoon salt
1/2 cup Vegetable Broth or Chicken Broth,
    pages 152-153, canned broth or water
1/4 cup bottled clam juice
1/4 cup dry sherry
1/2 cup evaporated skim milk
1 tablespoon fresh lemon juice
3 teaspoons peanut oil or vegetable oil
2 (4-oz.) sole fillets

1 small onion, chopped
1/2 small green bell pepper, chopped
2 celery stalks, thinly sliced
1/2 lb. large shrimp, peeled, deveined,
    coarsely chopped
2 to 3 dashes hot-pepper sauce
Salt
Freshly ground black pepper
2 cups hot cooked rice
Minced fresh parsley

In a medium bowl, combine cornstarch, mustard and salt; stir in 1/4 cup broth or water to make a smooth paste. Gradually add clam juice, sherry and milk; add lemon juice, stirring to blend. Set mixture aside. Using 1/2 teaspoon oil, lightly oil bottom and side of wok; place over high heat. When hot, add fillets in a single layer. Cook 1 minute; turn and cook other side 1 minute. Pour in remaining 1/4 cup broth or water; cover and steam 1 minute or until fish is opaque and flakes easily with a fork. Remove wok from heat; transfer fillets to a warm plate. Keep fish warm. If necessary, wipe wok clean with paper towels; add remaining 2-1/2 teaspoons oil. Place over medium-high heat; add onion, bell pepper and celery. Stir-fry 1 minute or until vegetables are crisp-tender. Stir in shrimp; stir-fry until pink. Add cornstarch mixture to wok, stirring until slightly thickened. Break cooked fish fillets into bite-sized pieces; stir into wok. Season to taste with hot-pepper sauce, salt and black pepper. Stir until sauce is hot. Serve over hot cooked rice. Garnish with parsley. Makes 4 servings.

About 290 calories per serving.

Oriental Steamed Fish

Steamed fish retains all of its natural moisture and flavor; it's simple to prepare and very delicious.

1 small lemon, cut in thin slices
2 cucumbers, peeled, seeded,
  cut in thin slices
6 small radishes, cut in thin slices
1 teaspoon salt
1 (1-1/2-lb.) sea bass or other firm fish

3 tablespoons fresh lemon juice
1 tablespoon mirin
1 tablespoon soy sauce
2 tablespoons minced fresh parsley
1 tablespoon minced green-onion tops
Parsley sprigs

Cut 1/2 the lemon slices into wedges; cut other slices in 1/2. Place cucumber and radish slices in a small bowl; sprinkle with salt. Toss to coat evenly. Add enough cold water and ice cubes to cover. Refrigerate several hours or until ready to use. Sprinkle cavity of fish with 1 tablespoon lemon juice, 1-1/2 teaspoons mirin or wine, and 1-1/2 teaspoons soy sauce. With a small knife, cut 1/4-inch slashes down body of fish, spacing slashes about 1/2 inch apart; insert a lemon wedge in each slash. Sprinkle 1 tablespoon lemon juice, remaining mirin or wine, and remaining soy sauce over top of fish. Place fish in a shallow steamer dish on a rack in a wok over boiling water. Cover and steam 12 to 15 minutes or until fish is opaque through the center. Do not overcook as fish will continue to cook from residual heat after removed from wok. Let fish stand on a cooling rack about 15 minutes. Pour off accumulated liquid. Cover and seal dish with plastic wrap. Refrigerate until chilled.

To serve, in a small bowl, combine minced parsley, green-onion tops and remaining 1 tablespoon lemon juice. Spread mixture over fish. Arrange lemon slices overlapping down center of fish. Place fish on a serving platter. Drain cucumber and radish slices, then blot dry with paper towels; arrange around fish. Garnish platter with parsley sprigs. Serve cold. Makes 3 servings.

About 240 calories per serving.

Mirin is a syrupy sweet rice wine used for cooking and glazing foods. It adds an interesting and different sweet flavor. It is expensive but keeps well and a little goes a long way. Substitute saké or other rice wine heated with an equal amount of sugar until thick and syrupy.

Mexican-Style Haddock

A perfect dish for those dining alone or when only one in the family is counting calories.

Salt
1 (4-oz.) haddock fillet
1/4 teaspoon pure chili powder
1 onion slice
1 tomato slice

1 tablespoon lime juice
2 tablespoons Vegetable Broth, page 152,
   or water
Minced fresh parsley

Place wok over high heat; sprinkle lightly with salt. When hot, salt will darken slightly. Add fish fillet. Cook until lightly browned; turn and sprinkle with 1/4 teaspoon salt and chili powder. Cover with onion and tomato slices. Cook 30 seconds or until lightly browned. Sprinkle with lime juice; add broth or water. Cover and steam 1 minute. Uncover and cook until fish is opaque and flakes easily with a fork. Garnish with parsley. Serve immediately. Makes 1 serving.

About 110 calories per serving.

Flounder with Seasoned Rice

Oriental fish sauce, known as patis, *is available in Oriental stores or gourmet markets.*

1/4 teaspoon saffron threads, crumbled
1/2 cup medium-dry sherry
1 (6-oz.) pkg. frozen edible pea pods
2 teaspoons peanut oil or vegetable oil
1 small red onion, chopped
3 cups water
1 cup Italian short-grain rice

1/2 teaspoon salt
1/4 teaspoon freshly ground black pepper
1/4 teaspoon Oriental fish sauce, if desired
1 (12-oz.) pkg. individually frozen
   flounder fillets, thawed
Paprika

In a small bowl, sprinkle saffron into sherry. Place pea pods in a second small bowl; cover with 1 cup boiling water. Let stand 1 minute; drain and blot dry with paper towels. Place wok over high heat; add oil. When hot, add onion; stir-fry about 1 minute. Add 3 cups water, saffron, sherry and rice. Season with salt, pepper and fish sauce, if desired. Bring to a boil. Reduce heat; cover and simmer 20 minutes or until rice is tender and almost all liquid is absorbed. Stir pea pods into rice. Remove wok from heat. Top with fish fillets. Cover and steam 5 minutes or until fish is opaque and flakes easily with a fork. Rice mixture will be slightly soupy. Serve while hot in large shallow bowls. Sprinkle with paprika. Makes 4 servings.

About 280 calories per serving.

tip

Italian short-grain rice may be sold under the name of Arborio rice.

VEGETABLES & SALADS

Stir-frying fresh vegetables in a little oil or stir-steaming them in their own juice helps to bring out the natural flavor. Vegetables will require little or no seasoning after cooking. You can stir-fry one vegetable with as much success as you can stir-fry a blend of vegetables.

Much has been written about preparing vegetables for stir-frying. You may have been told that this is difficult and time-consuming, but it is not. Vegetables are either sliced, chopped, diced or minced so that as much cut surface as possible will be exposed to the heat. This allows them to cook in a short time. Refer to pages 6-8 for information on vegetable preparation.

Many people fail to stay on a diet because they become bored—disenchanted by the limited selection of food and stymied by the limited ways they know how to prepare it. Warm salads and those that mix hot and cold ingredients are never boring, but flavorful and different from traditional lettuce, tomato and dressing. When you stop to think that chilling dulls the flavor in most foods just as heat brings it out, you can understand the reasons why a mixture of hot and cold food perks up your taste buds. And such salads are so easy to prepare.

The basic idea for these salads can be adapted to salad greens and other ingredients you have on hand. They're quick and easy and taste positively divine.

Menu

Breakfast
1 omelet made with 1 egg and 1 egg white
1 fresh peach
2 wassa bread crackers   1 teaspoon margarine
Coffee or tea
Snack
1 apple
Lunch
Stir-Fried Chicken Salad, page 114
2 flatbread crackers
Iced tea with mint
Dinner
Spinach & Ricotta-Stuffed Tomatoes, page 111
2 bread sticks
Seafood Quenelles with Vegetables, page 80
Tropical Cheesecake with Fruit Topping, page 145
Snack
1 cup Chicken Broth, page 153   Tofu Croutons, page 151

About 1200 calories

VEGETABLE STEAMING CHART

Vegetable	Minutes
Asparagus, medium stalks, whole	6 to 8
Green beans, whole, fresh	10
frozen (10-oz.) pkg.	12
Bean Sprouts	2 to 3
Beets, medium, whole	25 to 30
Broccoli flowerets, stems 3/8 inch thick	6 to 7
Brussels sprouts, medium, whole	9
Cabbage, green, 1-1/2 lbs., quartered	15
Cabbage, green, shredded;	10
in shallow baking dish	
Cabbage, green, cut in eight wedges	11
Carrots, medium (4 oz. each), whole	15
Carrots, thinly sliced	5
Cauliflower, separated into flowerets	8 to 10
Corn, freshly shucked, whole	5 to 7
Eggplant, 1 lb., cut in half lengthwise	13
Mushrooms, 1/4-inch	5
Onions, 1-1/2 inch, whole;	12
3- to 4-inch, quartered	12
Peas, green, shelled	5 to 7
Peppers, bell, red or green,	
cut in 1/2-inch strips	4 to 5
Potatoes, new, red-skinned, small	15 to 20
Potatoes, sweet or yams (6 oz. each)	25 to 30
Snow peas or other edible pea pods, whole	4 to 5
Squash, acorn, 1-1/2 lbs., cut in half	20 to 25
Squash, butternut, 1-1/2 lbs., cut in half	20 to 25
Squash, zucchini or yellow summer,	
whole, 1-1/2 inches in diameter	8
Squash, zucchini or yellow summer, 1/2-inch slices	5
Turnips, white, medium (3 oz. each)	25 to 30

Steamed Asparagus with Butter Sauce

Use this flavorful sauce over any other steamed vegetable.

16 to 20 thin asparagus spears

Low-Calorie Butter Sauce:

2 tablespoons dry white wine
2 tablespoons white-wine vinegar
2 tablespoons chilled butter, in 1 piece

1 tablespoon evaporated skim milk
Salt
Freshly ground black pepper

To cook asparagus, break tough ends from asparagus; rinse under cold running water. Place asparagus in a single layer on a rack in a wok over simmering water. Cover and steam 6 to 8 minutes or until crisp-tender.

For sauce, in a small saucepan, combine wine and vinegar; simmer over low heat, uncovered, until reduced by about 1/2. Increase heat to high; when liquid boils, add butter and milk. Stir until butter is partially melted; remove from heat. Let stand until butter has completely melted; stir to blend. Season to taste with salt and pepper.

To complete, transfer cooked asparagus to a serving platter. Top with warm sauce. Makes 2 servings.

About 140 calories per serving.

Italian-Style Steamed Asparagus

Plain steamed asparagus is great — this simple Italian version is magnificent.

1/4 cup dry bread crumbs
2 tablespoons grated Parmesan cheese
1/8 teaspoon salt
16 to 20 thin asparagus spears,
  about 1 lb.

2 tablespoons Vegetable Broth,
  page 152, or water

In a small bowl, combine bread crumbs, cheese and salt. Break tough ends from asparagus; rinse under cold running water. Place asparagus spears in a shallow dish; place on a rack in a wok over simmering water. Cover and steam 6 to 8 minutes or until crisp-tender. Top with bread-crumb mixture; sprinkle with broth or water. Cover and steam 30 seconds. Makes 4 servings.

About 50 calories per serving.

95

Curried Cauliflower & Broccoli

A colorful combination of broccoli and cauliflower — tastes as great as it looks.

1/4 cup low-fat ricotta cheese
1 teaspoon plain low-fat yogurt
1/8 teaspoon salt
1 tablespoon mango chutney, finely chopped

1/2 to 1 teaspoon curry powder
1 cup cauliflowerets
1 cup broccoli flowerets

In a food processor fitted with a metal blade, combine cheese and yogurt; process until smooth. Scrape into a small bowl; stir in salt, chutney and curry powder to taste. Place cauliflower and broccoli on a steamer rack in a wok over simmering water. Cover and steam 5 to 6 minutes or until crisp-tender. Transfer to a serving bowl. Stir in cheese mixture until vegetables are evenly coated. Makes 4 servings.

About 50 calories per serving.

Cauliflower with Cheese & Chili

Bored with plain steamed vegetables? Try this combination and enjoy.

1/4 cup low-fat ricotta cheese
2 tablespoons evaporated skim milk
2 cups cauliflowerets

Salt
About 1 teaspoon pure chili powder

In a small bowl, stir together cheese and milk. Place cauliflowerets on a rack in a wok over simmering water; cover and steam 5 to 8 minutes or until crisp-tender. Season to taste with salt. Place in a serving bowl. Stir in cheese mixture. Sprinkle liberally with chili powder. Makes 4 servings.

About 45 calories per serving.

Stir-Fried Tomatoes with Capers

One of the best ways I know to add flavor excitement to tomatoes.

3 large tomatoes
3 tablespoons capers, drained

Salt
Freshly ground black pepper

Bring a small saucepan of water to a boil. Plunge each tomato into boiling water 10 to 15 seconds. Hold each tomato under cold running water and peel off skin. Remove and discard cores. Cut tomatoes into large chunks, reserving juice. Place wok over high heat. When hot, add tomato chunks with juice; stir-fry about 1 minute. Sprinkle with capers. Season to taste with salt and pepper. Serve hot. Makes 4 servings.

About 20 calories per serving.

Celery & Tomato Stir-Fry with Beans

Wonderfully satisfying, nutritionally sound and, best of all, very delicious.

4 tomatoes
1 small hot red or green chili
2 teaspoons peanut oil or vegetable oil
1 onion, chopped
1 small garlic clove, minced
2 cups (1/4-inch) celery slices
1 tablespoon fresh basil leaves, chopped,
  or 1 teaspoon dried leaf basil
1/2 teaspoon dried leaf oregano
1/4 teaspoon dried leaf tarragon

2 cups cooked white kidney beans
2 tablespoons Vegetable Broth,
  page 152, or water
2 teaspoons tarragon vinegar
1/2 teaspoon sugar
1/2 teaspoon salt
1/4 teaspoon freshly ground black pepper
1/2 cup chopped celery leaves
2 cups hot cooked rice

Plunge each tomato into boiling water 30 seconds; hold under cold running water and slip off skins. Cut tomatoes into chunks, reserving juice. Trim hot chili; hold under cold running water and remove seeds. Finely dice chili. Place wok over high heat; add oil. When hot, add onion; stir-fry about 1 minute. Stir in garlic and chili; stir-fry 30 seconds. Add celery; stir-fry about 1 minute. Stir in tomato chunks with juice, basil, oregano, tarragon, beans, broth or water, vinegar, sugar, salt and pepper. Cover and steam 1 minute. Stir in celery leaves. Serve over hot cooked rice. Makes 4 servings.

About 280 calories per serving.

How to Make Stir-Fried Cucumbers

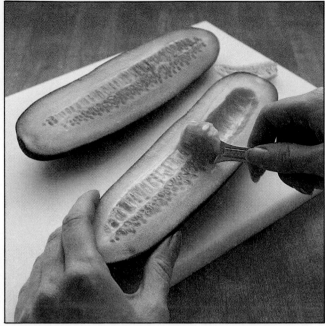 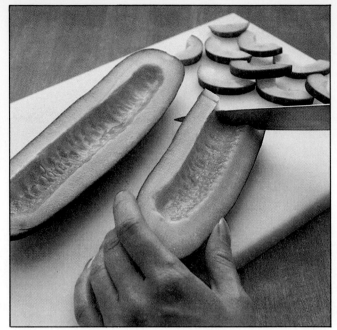

1/Cut cucumber in 1/2 lengthwise; scoop out seeds.

2/Cut cucumber crosswise into thin slices.

Stir-Fried Cucumbers

A colorful, flavorful mix.

1 large cucumber
1 large red bell pepper, cut in thin strips
1 small onion, chopped
2 tablespoons Vegetable Broth,
  page 152, or water

1 teaspoon sesame oil
1 tablespoon saké or dry sherry
Salt
Freshly ground black pepper

Peel cucumber if waxed; cut in 1/2 lengthwise. Scoop out seeds; cut crosswise into thin slices. Place wok over high heat. When hot, add bell pepper and onion; stir-fry 30 seconds. Add cucumber, then sprinkle with broth or water; cover and steam 1 minute. Stir-fry until vegetables are crisp-tender. Stir in sesame oil and wine or sherry. Season to taste with salt and black pepper. Makes 4 servings.

About 40 calories per serving.

Pea Pods with Water Chestnuts

Sugar-snap peas, snow peas or Chinese pea pods can be used in this colorful dish.

2 teaspoons peanut oil or vegetable oil
1 (10-oz) pkg. frozen edible pea pods or
   1 lb. fresh edible pea pods, trimmed
1 tablespoon minced shallots

1/2 cup sliced water chestnuts
Salt
Freshly ground black pepper

Place wok over medium heat; add oil. When hot, add pea pods, shallots and water chestnuts. Stir-fry 1 to 2 minutes for frozen pea pods or 2 to 3 minutes for fresh pea pods. Season to taste with salt and pepper. Makes 4 servings.

About 60 calories per serving.

Sweet & Sour Cabbage with Apples & Ham

A zesty cabbage combination served over rice.

1 tablespoon cider vinegar
1 tablespoon soy sauce
1 teaspoon sugar
1/4 to 1/2 teaspoon dried red-pepper flakes,
   crushed
1 tablespoon cornstarch
2 teaspoons peanut oil or vegetable oil
1/4 lb. lean cooked ham,
   cut in 1/2-inch strips

1 lb. green cabbage, coarsely chopped
2 crisp tart apples, such as Granny Smith,
   peeled, coarsely chopped
1 garlic clove, minced, if desired
1/2 cup Chicken Broth or Vegetable Broth,
   pages 152-153, canned broth or water
Salt
Freshly ground black pepper
2 cups hot cooked rice

In a small bowl, stir together vinegar, soy sauce, sugar, red-pepper flakes and cornstarch; set aside. Place wok over high heat; add oil. When hot, add ham strips; stir-fry 30 seconds. Add cabbage, apples and garlic, if desired; stir-fry 1 minute. Stir in broth; cover and steam 2 to 3 minutes or until cabbage is nearly crisp-tender. Stir cornstarch mixture into cabbage mixture. Cook, stirring constantly, until liquid boils and thickens. Season to taste with salt and black pepper. Serve over hot cooked rice. Makes 4 servings.

About 270 calories per serving.

Three-Squash Stir-Fry

A great recipe to make when squash is at its peak season.

3 tomatoes
1 small hot red or green chili
2 teaspoons peanut oil or vegetable oil
1 large onion, chopped
1 small garlic clove, minced
3 yellow summer squash,
  cut in 1/2-inch cubes
3 zucchini, cut in 1/4-inch sticks

3 pattypan squash, thinly sliced
1 cup fresh or frozen whole-kernel corn
1 Belgian endive, thinly sliced, or
  1 cup shredded bok choy or
  Chinese cabbage
Salt
Freshly ground black pepper
2 cups hot cooked rice

Cut tomatoes into chunks, reserving juice. Trim hot chili; hold under cold running water and remove seeds. Finely dice chili; stir into tomatoes. Place wok over high heat; add oil. When hot, add onion; stir-fry 1 minute. Stir in garlic; stir-fry about 30 seconds. Add yellow squash, zucchini and pattypan squash; stir-fry about 1 minute. Stir in tomatoes with juice and chili. Cover and steam 1 minute. Stir in corn and endive, bok choy or cabbage; stir-fry 30 seconds. Season to taste with salt and black pepper. Serve over hot cooked rice. Makes 4 servings.

About 240 calories per serving.

Southern Stir-Steamed Summer Squash

A Charleston classic, with fewer calories.

4 or 5 small yellow summer squash
1 small onion, chopped
2 tablespoons Vegetable Broth,
  page 152, or water
1 tablespoon butter
1 teaspoon sugar

1/4 teaspoon salt
Pinch of ground cinnamon
Pinch of ground nutmeg
Pinch of ground ginger
Pinch of ground allspice

Cut squash at a 45-degree angle into thin, uniform ovals. Place wok over medium-high heat. When hot, add squash and onion; stir-fry about 1 minute. Sprinkle with broth or water; add butter, sugar, salt and spices. Cover and steam 1 minute. Stir-fry until squash is crisp-tender. Makes 4 servings.

About 50 calories per serving.

Stir-Fried Zucchini

A stir-fry so quick and easy, it will amaze you.

4 or 5 small zucchini
Salt

Freshly ground black pepper

Cut zucchini at a 45-degree angle into thin, uniform ovals. Place wok over high heat. When hot, add zucchini; stir-fry, tossing slices up against the side of the wok, then scooping them back down toward center. When slices begin to be flecked with brown, lightly sprinkle with salt to taste. Continue to stir-fry, tossing slices as you would toss a salad, but more rapidly, until they are evenly flecked with brown on both sides and become almost translucent. Entire cooking time should be no more than about 4 minutes. Season to taste with pepper. Makes 4 servings.

About 14 calories per serving.

Zucchini in Orange Sauce

A new flavor for a familiar vegetable.

About 1 teaspoon peanut oil or
** vegetable oil**
4 to 6 small zucchini, thinly sliced
2 tablespoons Vegetable Broth,
** page 152, or water**

1/2 cup fresh orange juice
1 teaspoon grated orange peel
Salt

Lightly oil bottom and side of wok; place over high heat. When hot, add zucchini; stir-fry 1 minute. Sprinkle with broth or water; cover and steam 1 minute. Add orange juice and orange peel. Cook, stirring constantly, until sauce is reduced and slightly thickens. Season to taste with salt. Makes 4 servings.

About 50 calories per serving.

How to Make Glazed Steamed Onions

1/Cut off end of each onion; squeeze to slip off skin.

2/Stir cornstarch mixture until thickened to a smooth glaze; pour over cooked onions.

Glazed Steamed Onions

Glistening onions to add sparkle to your diet.

16 fresh pearl onions
1/2 cup Chicken Broth or Vegetable Broth,
   pages 152-153, canned broth or water
2 tablespoons apple brandy or apple jack

2 teaspoons cornstarch
1 teaspoon sugar
Salt

In a small saucepan of water, boil unpeeled onions 3 minutes. Rinse in cold water and drain. Cut off end of each onion; squeeze to slip off skin. Place onions in a single layer in a steamer dish. Place dish on a rack in a wok over simmering water. Cover and steam until onions are easily pierced; remove from wok. Pour liquid from wok; wipe dry with paper towels. In wok, combine broth or water and brandy; stir in cornstarch and sugar until smooth. Season lightly with salt. Place over medium heat; bring to a simmer. Stir until mixture thickens to a smooth glaze; pour over onions. Makes 4 servings.

About 90 calories per serving.

Stir-Steamed Onions

Onion slices will separate into rings as you stir-fry.

**3 large Vidalia, red or
  other sweet onions, thinly sliced**
**About 2 tablespoons Vegetable Broth,
  page 152, or water**

Salt
Freshly ground black pepper

Place wok over high heat. When hot, add onions; stir-fry about 1 minute. Sprinkle with broth or water; cover and steam 1 minute. Stir-fry onions until tender and liquid has evaporated. Season to taste with salt and pepper. Makes 4 servings.

About 35 calories per serving.

Peppers, Onions & Mushrooms

A great dish to serve in the summer with grilled chicken.

1/4 lb. mushrooms, thinly sliced
2 onions, thinly sliced
**1 large green bell pepper,
  cut in thin strips**

**2 tablespoons Vegetable Broth,
  page 152, or water**
Salt
Freshly ground black pepper

Place wok over high heat. When hot, add mushrooms, onions and bell pepper; stir-fry about 1 minute. Sprinkle with broth or water; cover and steam 1 minute or until mushrooms give off some liquid. Stir-fry until vegetables are crisp-tender. Season to taste with salt and black pepper. Makes 4 servings.

About 35 calories per serving.

Chili in Pepper Boats

Delicious Mexican chili flavor without the added calories from meat.

4 large green bell peppers
2 teaspoons peanut oil or vegetable oil
1 garlic clove, crushed
1 tablespoon pure chili powder
1/4 teaspoon ground cumin
1/4 teaspoon ground oregano
1/4 teaspoon ground coriander
1 (16-oz.) can whole peeled tomatoes
1 large Vidalia onion or
    other sweet onion, chopped

2 cups canned red kidney beans
1/4 cup chopped green olives
Salt
Freshly ground black pepper
1-1/2 to 2 cups mung bean sprouts, rinsed,
    drained, blotted dry
1/2 cup shredded Monterey Jack
    cheese (2 oz.)

Cut a thick slice from 1 side of each bell pepper, reserving pepper slices; scoop out and discard seeds to form pepper boats. Finely dice reserved pepper slices. Place pepper boats on a rack in a wok over simmering water. Cover and steam 5 minutes or until tender; remove and set aside. Clean wok and wipe dry with paper towels. Place wok over high heat; add oil. When hot, add garlic; stir-fry until lightly browned. Remove and discard garlic. Add diced bell pepper to wok; stir-fry 1 minute. Stir in chili powder, cumin, oregano, coriander and tomatoes with juice. Stir, breaking up tomatoes; bring mixture to a simmer. Stir in onion, kidney beans and olives; cover and simmer 5 minutes. Season to taste with salt and black pepper. Place pepper boats on small plates. Surround each bell pepper with bean sprouts; fill with chili mixture, letting excess spill over onto sprouts. Sprinkle with shredded cheese. Makes 4 servings.

About 290 calories per serving.

Classic Mixed-Vegetable Stir-Fry

A good-tasting and low-calorie dish—great to serve with grilled chicken or fish.

1 teaspoon peanut oil or vegetable oil
1 Vidalia onion or other sweet onion,
    chopped
1 small green bell pepper, chopped
2 celery stalks, sliced
2 teaspoons fresh lemon juice

1 tablespoon soy sauce
4 large mushrooms, quartered
1/4 head bok choy or savoy cabbage,
    shredded
1/2 cup mung bean sprouts, rinsed,
    drained, blotted dry

Place wok over high heat; add oil. When hot, add onion, bell pepper, celery; stir-fry 1 minute or until slightly shiny from their own juices. Sprinkle evenly with lemon juice and soy sauce; cover and steam 30 seconds. Add mushrooms, bok choy or cabbage, and bean sprouts; continue to stir-fry until vegetables are crisp-tender. Makes 4 servings.

About 50 calories per serving.

Chili in Pepper Boats

Vegetable-Garden Stir-Fry

The freshest and best from your garden.

1 cup broccoli flowerets
1 cup cauliflowerets
2 to 3 tablespoons Vegetable Broth or
  Chicken Broth, pages 152-153,
  canned broth or water
1 small zucchini, thickly sliced

1 small yellow summer squash,
  thickly sliced
2 tablespoons minced green onion
Salt
Freshly ground black pepper
1 tablespoon minced fresh parsley

Light & Lemony Sauce:
2 teaspoons cornstarch
3/4 cup Vegetable Broth or Chicken Broth,
  pages 152-153, canned broth or water
1/2 cup evaporated skim milk
1 egg yolk

2 to 3 drops hot-pepper sauce
1 tablespoon fresh lemon juice
1 tablespoon butter, room temperature
Salt
Freshly ground black pepper

For sauce, in a small saucepan, stir together cornstarch and 1/4 cup broth or water until smooth; add remaining broth and milk. Bring mixture to a full boil over medium heat, stirring constantly, 1 to 2 minutes or until slightly thickened. Remove from heat. Beat egg yolk until blended; stir in 1/4 cup hot thickened broth mixture until blended. Add egg mixture to remaining hot mixture, stirring rapidly as added. Place saucepan over low heat. Season with hot-pepper sauce and lemon juice. Add butter; stir until sauce is heated through. Season to taste with salt and black pepper; keep warm while cooking vegetables.

To cook vegetables, lightly oil bottom and side of wok; place over high heat. When hot, add broccoli and cauliflowerets; stir-fry about 1 minute. Sprinkle with broth or water; cover and steam 1 minute or until vegetables give off some liquid. Add zucchini and yellow squash; stir-fry, covering wok occasionally, about 1 minute or until vegetables are crisp-tender. Pour in warm sauce; sprinkle with green onion. Season to taste with salt and black pepper; garnish with parsley. Makes 4 servings.

About 120 calories per serving.

Fruit & Vegetable Stir-Fry

This recipe makes a plain stir-fry into an extra-special dish.

1 orange	4 large mushrooms, quartered
1 teaspoon soy sauce	2 celery stalks, thinly sliced
1 teaspoon tarragon vinegar or	1/2 small green bell pepper,
white-wine vinegar	cut in thin strips
1/2 teaspoon sesame oil	1 small tart apple, peeled, diced
1 teaspoon peanut oil or vegetable oil	1/4 head green cabbage, finely shredded
1 small onion, chopped	1/2 cup seedless green grapes

Peel orange; holding it over a food-processor bowl or blender container, cut into chunks, letting chunks and juice fall into bowl or container. Add soy sauce, vinegar and sesame oil. Process orange mixture to a chunky sauce; set aside. Place wok over high heat; add 1 teaspoon peanut oil or vegetable oil. When hot, add onion, mushrooms, celery, bell pepper and apple; stir-fry about 1 minute. Cover and steam 30 seconds. Add orange sauce, cabbage and grapes; stir-fry until vegetables are crisp-tender and grapes are heated through. Makes 4 servings.

About 90 calories per serving.

Hawaiian Vegetables

A colorful combination to serve anytime.

1 (8-oz.) can pineapple chunks in	1/4 teaspoon dried leaf basil
unsweetened juice	1/4 teaspoon ground ginger
8 large mushrooms, sliced	1/2 teaspoon curry powder
1 small green bell pepper, chopped	2 oz. lean cooked ham, cut in thin strips
1 small red bell pepper, chopped	1/2 cup drained, chopped water chestnuts
1 onion, diced	Salt
1 sweet potato, steam-cooked, peeled, sliced	2 cups hot cooked rice

Drain pineapple, reserving juice. Place wok over low heat. Add mushrooms, bell peppers and onion; sprinkle with a few tablespoons pineapple juice. Steam-stir until mushrooms give off some liquid. Increase heat to high; stir-fry until vegetables are crisp-tender. Add pineapple, sweet potato, basil, ginger, curry powder, ham and water chestnuts. Season to taste with salt. Stir-fry until ingredients are hot. Serve over hot cooked rice. Makes 4 servings.

About 240 calories per serving.

Vegetable Curry

Hot and spicy; a feast for everyone.

2 teaspoons cornstarch
1 cup Vegetable Broth, page 152, or water
1/2 small lemon
1 small onion
1 teaspoon peanut oil or vegetable oil
1/4 lb. mushrooms, sliced
1/4 lb. young green beans
1 cup cauliflowerets
1 cup broccoli flowerets

1 small yellow summer squash,
  cut in thick slices
About 1 teaspoon curry powder
1/2 teaspoon Quatre Epices, page 155
1/2 cup fresh or thawed frozen green peas
1 tablespoon mango chutney, finely chopped
About 1/4 teaspoon salt
Freshly ground black pepper
2 cups hot cooked rice

In a small bowl, stir together cornstarch and broth or water until smooth; set aside. Remove colored peel from lemon; cut into julienne strips. Place lemon-peel strips in a small saucepan; add 2 cups water. Simmer over low heat 15 minutes; drain and set aside. Squeeze juice from lemon; set aside. Cut onion into wedges; separate wedges into pieces. Lightly oil bottom and side of wok; place over high heat. When hot, add onion pieces and mushrooms; stir-fry 1 minute. Cover and steam 30 seconds or until mushrooms give off some liquid. Remove onion and mushrooms from wok, leaving cooking liquid in wok. Add green beans, cauliflower and broccoli; stir-fry about 2 minutes. Add squash; stir-fry about 1 minute. Stir in cooked onion, mushrooms, curry powder and Quatre Epices. Add reserved lemon juice. Stir cornstarch mixture into vegetable mixture. Stir in peas, chutney and lemon peel. Stirring over medium heat, cook until sauce thickens. Season to taste with salt and pepper. Serve over hot cooked rice. Garnish with tomato roses or as desired. Serve with desired condiments, such as chopped green onions, diced cucumber and diced tomato. Makes 4 servings.

About 210 calories per serving.

Vegetable Curry

Tabbouleh-Stuffed Tomatoes

Tabbouleh is a Middle Eastern salad made with bulgur.

1/2 cup bulgur	Salt
1/3 cup finely chopped green onions	Freshly ground black pepper
1/4 cup minced radishes	1 egg yolk
1/3 cup raisins	4 large tomatoes
1/4 cup fresh lemon juice	Small romaine leaves or other lettuce leaves
1 tablespoon olive oil	1 tablespoon chopped fresh mint or
	1/4 cup minced fresh parsley

Place bulgur in a medium bowl; add boiling water to cover by 1 inch. Cover and let stand 1 hour or until water has been absorbed. Place bulgur on a clean towel; roll up and squeeze thoroughly to remove excess water. Transfer to a medium bowl; fluff with a fork. Add green onions, radishes, raisins, lemon juice and olive oil. Season to taste with salt and pepper. Stir in egg yolk, blending well. Cover and let stand 30 minutes. Cut a thick slice from top of each tomato. With a small spoon, carefully scoop out tomato pulp, reserving pulp; lightly sprinkle tomato shells with salt. Turn shells, cut-side down, on double paper towels to drain 30 minutes. Chop tomato pulp and tops; stir into bulgur mixture. Blot tomato shells dry with paper towels. Fill tomato shells with bulgur mixture, pressing mixture down into shells. Place stuffed tomato shells in a flat steamer dish on a rack in a wok over simmering water. Cover and steam 10 minutes or until tomatoes are soft, but not falling apart. Remove dish from wok; place on a cooling rack. Cool to room temperature. Line 4 plates with lettuce; place tomatoes on lined plates. Garnish with mint or parsley. Serve at room temperature. Makes 4 servings.

About 180 calories per serving.

How to Make Tabbouleh-Stuffed Tomatoes

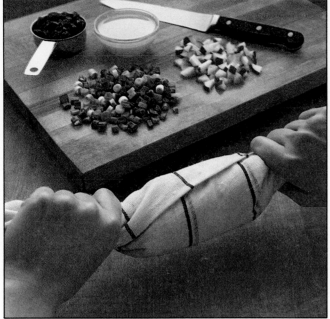

1/Drain bulgur; place soaked bulgur on a clean towel. Roll up and squeeze thoroughly to remove excess water.

2/Fill tomatoes with bulgur mixture, pressing mixture into shells. Place stuffed tomatoes on a flat steamer dish on a rack in a wok.

Spinach & Ricotta-Stuffed Tomatoes

A flavorful mid-summer dish when tomatoes are at their vine-ripened peak.

4 large tomatoes
Salt
1/2 cup low-fat ricotta cheese
1 tablespoon plain low-fat yogurt
1 teaspoon fresh lemon juice
Freshly ground black pepper

1 cup finely chopped onion
1 (10-oz.) pkg. thawed frozen spinach,
 drained
1 egg white
2 tablespoons toasted pine nuts

Cut a thick slice from top of each tomato. With a small spoon, carefully scoop out tomato pulp, reserving pulp; lightly sprinkle tomato shells with salt. Turn shells, cut-side down, on double paper towels to drain 30 minutes. Press pulp through a fine sieve into a small bowl, discarding seeds. In a large bowl, stir together cheese, yogurt and lemon juice. Season to taste with salt and pepper; set aside. Place wok over high heat. When hot, add strained tomato pulp and onion. Bring to a full boil; stir until almost all liquid has evaporated. Add spinach; stir-fry 1 to 2 minutes. Add spinach mixture to cheese mixture; blend well. In a small bowl, beat egg white until soft peaks form; fold into spinach-cheese mixture. Blot tomato shells dry with paper towels. Fill tomato shells with spinach mixture, pressing mixture down into shells. Garnish each with pine nuts. Place stuffed tomato shells in a flat steamer dish on a rack in a wok over simmering water. Cover and steam 10 minutes or until tomatoes are soft but not falling apart. Serve hot or at room temperature. Makes 4 servings.

About 130 calories per serving.

Southern-Style Potato Salad

Use this special diet mayonnaise with other favorite salads.

Salad:

2 teaspoons peanut oil or vegetable oil
1/4 cup thinly sliced celery
1/2 cup diced green bell pepper
1/4 cup diced red bell pepper
3 lb. small new potatoes

2 tablespoons Chicken Broth, page 153,
   canned broth or water
1 teaspoon salt
1 tablespoon minced chives

Low-Calorie Mayonnaise:

2 tablespoons low-fat ricotta cheese
1 tablespoon plain low-fat yogurt
1 egg yolk
1 teaspoon dry mustard
1/2 teaspoon salt
1/8 teaspoon white pepper

3 tablespoons peanut oil or vegetable oil,
   or 1-1/2 tablespoons peanut oil and
   1-1/2 tablespoons olive oil
1 teaspoon white-wine vinegar or
   tarragon vinegar
1 egg white

For salad, place wok over high heat; add 2 teaspoons oil. When hot, add celery and bell peppers; stir-fry until crisp-tender. Drain well; set aside. Wipe wok clean with paper towels. Place unpeeled potatoes on a rack in a wok over simmering water. Cover and steam until easily pierced. Cool potatoes slightly; slice into 1/2-inch rounds. Place in a large bowl; add broth or water. Stir gently until slices are evenly moistened and liquid has been absorbed. Fold in stir-fried celery mixture; cool mixture.

For dressing, in a blender or food processor fitted with a metal blade, combine cheese and yogurt; process until smooth. Add egg yolk, mustard, salt and white pepper. At low speed, gradually add oil through the feed tube or lid. As mixture thickens, add vinegar, a few drops at a time; blend 30 seconds. Scrape mixture into a large bowl. In a medium bowl, beat egg white until soft peaks form; fold into mayonnaise until blended.

To complete, add mayonnaise to salad; toss to blend. Garnish with chives. Serve at room temperature. Makes 8 servings.

About 230 calories per serving.

Warm Potato Salad with Green Beans

Serve with grilled fish for a delicious and easy meal.

Salad:

6 to 8 small new potatoes	Salt
1/2 lb. young green beans	2 green onions, thinly sliced
1 tablespoon white-wine vinegar	

Yogurt-Mustard Dressing:

1 tablespoon low-fat ricotta cheese	1/4 teaspoon Hungarian paprika
1/2 cup plain low-fat yogurt	Salt
1/2 teaspoon Dijon-style mustard	Freshly ground black pepper

For salad, place unpeeled potatoes on a rack in a wok over simmering water; cover and steam 5 minutes. Add green beans to rack. Cover and steam 6 to 8 minutes or until potatoes are easily pierced and green beans are crisp-tender; remove from wok.

For dressing, in a blender or food processor fitted with a metal blade, combine cheese, yogurt, mustard and paprika; process or blend until smooth. Season to taste with salt and pepper.

To complete, when potatoes are cool enough to handle, slice into a large bowl; add whole green beans. Sprinkle potatoes and beans with vinegar and salt to taste; toss until absorbed. Add dressing; toss to mix. Garnish with green onions. Makes 4 servings.

About 70 calories per serving.

Hot Bean Sprouts & Lettuce with Shrimp

By using ingredients that are available year-round, this salad could be called "Salad for all Seasons."

6 to 8 oz. cooked medium shrimp, peeled, deveined	2 tablespoons peanut oil or vegetable oil
1 small head iceberg lettuce	1 garlic clove, crushed
1 tablespoon tarragon vinegar or white-wine vinegar	1/2 lb. mung bean sprouts, rinsed, drained, blotted dry
1 teaspoon Dijon-style mustard	Salt
	Freshly ground black pepper

Pat shrimp thoroughly dry with paper towels. Use loose outer lettuce leaves to line salad plates or a bowl; tear remaining lettuce into bite-sized pieces. In a small bowl, combine vinegar and mustard. Place wok over high heat; add oil. When hot, add garlic; stir until lightly browned. Remove and discard garlic. Add lettuce pieces, bean sprouts and shrimp to wok; stir-fry 3 minutes or until sprouts are fragrant and shrimp are pink. Remove wok from heat. Add vinegar mixture to wok, tossing to blend. Season to taste with salt and pepper. Arrange warm salad on lettuce-lined plates or lined bowl. Serve immediately. Makes 4 servings.

About 140 calories per serving.

Stir-Fried Chicken Salad

A colorful, great tasting main-dish salad.

1 small head romaine,
  torn in bite-sized pieces
1 large tomato, cut in wedges
1 small Belgian endive, cored,
  cut in thin rounds
1 tablespoon peanut oil or vegetable oil
1/4 lb. young green beans

1 small green bell pepper,
  cut in thin strips
1/2 lb. boneless chicken breast, skinned,
  cut in bite-sized pieces
1 small fresh hot red pepper, seeded,
  minced, or 1/2 teaspoon dried red-pepper
  flakes, if desired

Dressing:

1 tablespoon olive oil
1/3 cup Chicken Broth, page 153,
  canned broth or water
1 garlic clove, split lengthwise
1 teaspoon minced fresh tarragon or
  1/4 teaspoon dried leaf tarragon
1 teaspoon minced fresh basil or
  1/4 teaspoon dried leaf basil

1 tablespoon minced fresh parsley
2 tablespoons sherry-wine vinegar or
  white-wine vinegar
1 teaspoon Dijon-style mustard
1/4 teaspoon salt
1/8 teaspoon freshly ground black pepper

For dressing, in a small bowl, combine olive oil, broth or water, garlic, tarragon, basil and parsley; let stand at room temperature about 1 hour. Stir in vinegar and mustard; season to taste with salt and black pepper.

For salad, in a large salad bowl, combine romaine, tomato and endive; cover and refrigerate until chilled. Place wok over high heat; add peanut or vegetable oil. When hot, add green beans, bell pepper and chicken; stir-fry until chicken is firm and white through center, and beans and bell pepper are crisp-tender. Remove wok from heat.

To complete, remove and discard garlic from prepared dressing; pour 1/2 the dressing over chicken and stir-fried vegetables. Toss to blend; let stand a few minutes to cool. To serve, pour remaining dressing over chilled greens and tomato strips; toss to blend. Drain chicken and stir-fried vegetables; arrange over greens mixture. Sprinkle with pepper flakes, if desired. Makes 4 servings.

Variation

Separate Belgian endive into leaves. Accent each plate with endive leaves.

About 170 calories per serving.

Zucchini & Broccoli Salad

Great for a salad luncheon or brunch.

1/2 lb. broccoli
2 tablespoons peanut oil or vegetable oil
2 zucchini, sliced
3 tablespoons red-wine vinegar
1 teaspoon minced fresh tarragon or
   1/4 teaspoon dried leaf tarragon
2 teaspoons minced fresh dill or
   3/4 teaspoon dill weed

Salt
Freshly ground black pepper
Crisp lettuce leaves
2 crisp tart red apples, unpeeled
2 tablespoons fresh lemon juice
About 1 cup cold water
4 cherry tomatoes, halved
Parsley sprigs

Break broccoli into flowerets, reserving stems. Chop flowerets; trim and cut stems into thin strips. Place wok over high heat; add oil. When hot, add broccoli stems and zucchini slices; stir-fry 1 minute. Add chopped broccoli; stir-fry 1 minute or until vegetables are crisp-tender. Remove wok from heat. Stir in vinegar, tarragon and dill. Season to taste with salt and pepper. Transfer to a bowl; cover and refrigerate until chilled. Line 4 salad plates with lettuce. Quarter apples; cut into thin slices. Place apple slices and lemon juice in a small bowl. Add enough cold water to cover. Drain chilled salad; arrange on lettuce-lined plates. Drain apple slices; arrange over each salad. Garnish with tomato halves and parsley sprigs. Makes 4 servings.

About 140 calories per serving.

Warm Beef Salad

Leftover cooked beef or pork can be used in this salad.

2 tablespoons olive oil
1 tablespoon tarragon vinegar
2 teaspoons Dijon-style mustard
About 1/2 teaspoon salt
Freshly ground black pepper

1 small head romaine
1 small bunch watercress
2 teaspoons peanut oil or vegetable oil
1/2 lb. thinly sliced cooked beef or pork

In a 1-cup measure, combine olive oil, vinegar and mustard. Season to taste with salt and pepper. Tear large romaine leaves into bite-sized pieces; leave small leaves whole. Remove and discard tough stems from watercress. Place wok over high heat; add peanut oil or vegetable oil. When hot, add beef or pork; stir-fry until heated through. Drain meat well over wok; then transfer to paper towels. Stir dressing mixture into wok. When hot, add torn lettuce and watercress; stir and toss until heated through. Remove wok from heat. Arrange seasoned romaine evenly on 2 large or 4 small plates. Top with meat slices; season lightly with additional salt and pepper. Makes 4 servings.

About 100 calories per serving.

Winter Vegetable Salad

Serve as a main course for lunch or as an appetite-appeasing first course for dinner.

Salad:

4 cups Vegetable Broth, page 152,
   or water
1 tablespoon red-wine vinegar or
   tarragon vinegar
1 teaspoon salt
4 small new potatoes, quartered
2 small white turnips, quartered

2 carrots, cut in 1-inch rounds
1 cup broccoli flowerets
1 cup cauliflowerets
1 (10-oz) pkg. frozen edible pea pods
Salt
Freshly ground black pepper
6 to 8 large crisp lettuce leaves

Creamy Cheese Dressing:

3 tablespoons low-fat ricotta cheese
2 tablespoons plain low-fat yogurt
2 tablespoons tarragon vinegar

2 teaspoons soy sauce
1 teaspoon Creole-style mustard
Freshly ground black pepper

For salad, place wok over high heat. Add broth or water, vinegar and 1 teaspoon salt; bring to a boil. Add potatoes, turnips and carrots; cook 5 minutes. Add broccoli and cauliflower; cook an additional 5 minutes. Remove vegetables with a slotted spoon to a large colander; set aside. Add pea pods to boiling water; boil 1 minute. Remove with slotted spoon; add to vegetables in colander.
For dressing, in a blender or food processor fitted with a metal blade, combine cheese and yogurt; process 30 seconds. Add vinegar, soy sauce, mustard and pepper; process until blended.
To complete, place cooked vegetables in a large bowl; toss with dressing. Season to taste with salt and pepper. Cover and refrigerate until chilled. Line 4 to 6 salad plates with lettuce leaves. Arrange salad on lettuce-lined plates. Makes 4 main-dish servings or 6 appetizer servings.

About 105 calories per main-dish serving, 70 calories per appetizer serving.

Warm Spinach-Almond Salad

Spinach salad is a favorite for many; try this version for variety.

1 lb. fresh spinach
2 tablespoons peanut oil or vegetable oil
2 tablespoons slivered almonds
1/4 lb. mushrooms, sliced

1/4 cup tarragon vinegar
1/2 teaspoon dried leaf tarragon
1/4 teaspoon salt
Freshly ground black pepper

Remove stems from spinach; wash under cold running water. Blot dry with paper towels. Tear into bite-sized pieces; place in a large bowl. Place wok over high heat; oil side and bottom of wok. When hot, add almonds; stir-fry until golden. Add mushrooms, vinegar, tarragon and salt; stir-fry until heated through. Pour over spinach; toss. Season with pepper. Makes 4 servings.

About 120 calories per serving.

Hawaiian Chicken Salad

An exceptionally easy way to prepare low-calorie, great-tasting sweet and sour chicken.

1 (8-oz.) can pineapple chunks in
  unsweetened juice
1 tablespoon cider vinegar
1 tablespoon low-calorie plum jelly
1 teaspoon cornstarch
2 teaspoons peanut oil or sesame oil

1 green bell pepper, cut in thin strips
1 lb. boneless chicken-breast halves,
  skinned, cut in 1-inch cubes
1/4 cup water
2 cups shredded lettuce

Drain pineapple, reserving juice. In a 2-cup measure, stir together pineapple juice, vinegar, plum jelly and cornstarch; set aside. Place wok over high heat; add oil. When hot, add bell pepper and chicken; stir-fry until chicken is firm and white through center. Reduce heat and add water; cover and steam 1 minute. Stir in pineapple. Add pineapple-juice mixture to wok; stir until blended and slightly thickened. Serve over shredded lettuce. Makes 4 servings.

About 220 calories per serving.

Terrific Turkey Salad

A beautiful salad and it can be prepared ahead.

4 raw turkey-breast slices, about 1 lb.,
  or 2 boneless chicken-breast halves
1/2 lb. mushrooms, thinly sliced
6 shallots, coarsely chopped
1/4 cup dry white wine
1/4 cup capers, drained
3 tablespoons Dijon-style mustard

1/2 teaspoon minced fresh tarragon or
  a pinch of dried leaf tarragon
Salt
Freshly ground black pepper
Crisp lettuce leaves
4 cherry tomatoes, halved
Watercress sprigs

Using the flat side of a cleaver or meat mallet, pound turkey or chicken pieces to flatten slightly; then cut into 1/4-inch strips. Place wok over high heat. When hot, add mushrooms and shallots; stir-fry 1 minute. Reduce heat; add wine and turkey or chicken strips. Simmer 4 to 5 minutes or until meat is firm and white through center. Add capers, mustard and tarragon. Season to taste with salt and pepper. Spoon turkey or chicken and liquid into a medium bowl; cool slightly. Drain and serve over crisp lettuce leaves. Garnish with tomato halves and watercress sprigs. Makes 4 servings.

About 180 calories per serving.

tip

If using cooked turkey, cook only until turkey is heated through.

PASTA & RICE

Pasta and rice are not excessively high in calories. Yes, you can include them in your diet. Like potatoes, pasta and rice have gained their bad reputation from what was served over them. The idea of pasta may create a picture of spaghetti in a thick, heavy tomato sauce. This is not what you will find in this book.

Pasta used in these recipes is made from semolina or vegetable flour. It is cooked only until it is *al dente*—tender but firm to the bite. For variety, use different types and shapes of pasta from long, thin linguine to short, flat noodles. Top cooked pasta with your choice of light, savory sauces. The results will be appreciated by your family and friends as a first course before a light entree or as a main dish for the meal. Either way, they are satisfying, but won't overdo the calories.

Rice was undoubtedly the first grain known to man—the staple diet of millions. It can be prepared and served in hundreds of different ways.

White long-grain rice is most popular. For variety, serve short plump Arborio rice from Italy or a long-grain Carolina rice. Other rices include brown rice, pecan rice, wild rice, native California long-grain rice and many different grains from the Near East, such as basmati. Each rice species has its own particular appetizing aroma and flavor. And learning to cook them is much easier than you may think.

Menu

Breakfast
1 egg and 1 egg white, scrambled
1 piece whole-wheat toast with 1 teaspoon margarine
1/2 grapefruit
Coffee or tea

Mid-Morning Snack
Coffee or tea   3 crackers

Lunch
Winter Vegetable Salad, page 117
1 oz. wheat crackers
Coffee or tea

Dinner
Pasta Primavera in a Wok, page 121
Italian Bread
6 oz. red wine
Apple-Spice Pudding Cake, page 149

Anytime Snack
1 apple   1 oz. Camembert cheese

About 1400 calories

Spaghetti with Tomato-Mushroom Sauce

Use your favorite thin spaghetti—capellini, fedelini or vermicelli.

1/4 teaspoon peanut oil or vegetable oil
1 (8-oz.) pkg. thin spaghetti
1 large onion, chopped
1/4 lb. mushrooms, chopped
2 tablespoons water
1 garlic clove, minced

2 cups Fresh Tomato Sauce or
   Quick Tomato Sauce, page 154,
   or canned tomato sauce
Salt
Freshly ground black pepper
2 tablespoons grated Parmesan cheese

In a large saucepan, bring 3 to 4 quarts water to a boil. Add oil and spaghetti; cook according to package directions until tender but firm to the bite. While pasta cooks, place wok over high heat. When hot, add onion and mushrooms; stir-fry 1 minute. Sprinkle with water and garlic; stir-fry 30 seconds. Cover and steam 1 minute or until mushrooms give off some liquid. Stir in tomato sauce; reduce heat and simmer 10 minutes. Season to taste with salt and pepper. Drain cooked pasta; add to sauce, stirring to blend. Serve hot garnished with cheese. Makes 4 servings.

About 280 calories per serving.

Pasta Shells with Zucchini

The shells catch and hold the flavorful sauce.

1/4 cup low-fat ricotta cheese
1/2 cup plain low-fat yogurt
3 tablespoons grated Parmesan cheese
1-1/4 teaspoons peanut oil or vegetable oil
1 (8-oz.) pkg. small pasta shells
2 medium zucchini, cut in thin strips

1 (12-oz.) can Italian-style peeled tomatoes
1 small garlic clove, minced
1 teaspoon Italian Seasoning, page 155
Salt
Freshly ground black pepper

In a small bowl, stir together ricotta cheese and 2 tablespoons yogurt until smooth; stir in remaining yogurt and 2 tablespoons Parmesan cheese. In a large saucepan, bring 3 to 4 quarts water to a boil. Add 1/4 teaspoon oil and pasta shells; cook according to package directions until tender but firm to the bite. While pasta cooks, lightly oil bottom and side of wok with remaining 1 teaspoon oil; place over high heat. When hot, add zucchini; stir-fry 1 minute. Drain and crush tomatoes, reserving juice. Add tomatoes, 1/4 cup reserved tomato juice, garlic and Italian Seasoning to zucchini; bring to a boil. Boil until liquid is reduced to about 1 tablespoon. Season to taste with salt and pepper. Remove wok from heat. Drain cooked pasta; stir cooked pasta shells and cheese-yogurt mixture into wok, tossing briefly. Serve hot, sprinkled with remaining 1 tablespoon Parmesan cheese. Makes 4 servings.

About 320 calories per serving.

Pasta Primavera in a Wok

Stir-steaming without oil allows the use of Parmesan cheese without adding too many calories.

1/4 teaspoon peanut oil or vegetable oil
1 (8-oz.) pkg. small pasta shells
1 small onion, chopped
1/4 lb. mushrooms, chopped
2 medium zucchini, thinly sliced
6 shallots, chopped
1 cup broccoli flowerets, chopped
2 tablespoons minced fresh basil or
  1 to 2 teaspoons dried leaf basil

1 teaspoon Italian Seasoning, page 155
1 (16-oz.) can crushed tomatoes with puree
  or 1 (16-oz.) can Italian-style
  tomatoes and 1 tablespoon tomato paste
Salt
Freshly ground black pepper
1/4 cup grated Parmesan cheese (3/4 oz.)

In a large saucepan, bring 3 to 4 quarts water to a boil. Add oil and pasta shells; cook according to package directions until tender but firm to the bite. While pasta cooks, prepare sauce. Place wok over high heat. When hot, add onion, mushrooms, zucchini and shallots; stir-fry 1 minute. Cover and steam 30 seconds. Add broccoli, basil, Italian Seasoning and tomatoes with juice or tomato paste. Reduce heat and simmer 5 minutes. Season to taste with salt and pepper. To serve, drain cooked pasta; place in a serving dish. Top with hot tomato sauce; sprinkle with cheese. Makes 4 servings.

About 310 calories per serving.

Pasta Topped with Zucchini & Cheese

A great way to enjoy pasta.

1 medium zucchini
2 teaspoons salt
2-1/4 teaspoons peanut oil or vegetable oil
1 tablespoon grated Parmesan cheese

1/2 teaspoon Italian Seasoning, if desired,
  page 155
1 (8-oz.) pkg. thin spaghetti or other pasta

Line a long, shallow baking dish with paper towels. Coarsely grate zucchini; spread in lined baking dish. Sprinkle with salt. Cover with additional paper towels. Over towels, place 1 or 2 heavy weights, such as scrubbed bricks wrapped securely in foil or 2 (1-pound) cans of vegetables. Let stand 20 to 30 minutes. Zucchini will release quite a bit of water. Place zucchini in a colander; rinse under cold water. Blot dry with paper towels. Place wok over high heat; add 2 teaspoons oil. When hot, add zucchini; stir-fry 1 minute. Don't overcook; zucchini should remain crisp. Transfer to a medium bowl; cool to room temperature. Stir in cheese and Italian Seasoning, if desired. In a large saucepan, bring 3 to 4 quarts water to a boil. Add remaining 1/4 teaspoon oil and pasta; cook according to package directions until tender but firm to the bite. Drain cooked pasta. To serve, top cooked pasta with zucchini-cheese mixture. Makes 4 servings.

About 240 calories per serving.

Vegetable Lo Mein

Don't let names bother you—call this Linguine in Cheese Sauce with Vegetables *if you prefer.*

2-1/4 teaspoons peanut oil or vegetable oil
1 (8-oz.) pkg. linguine or other thin pasta
3/4 cup low-fat ricotta cheese
2 tablespoons grated Parmesan cheese
1/2 small cauliflower
1/2 bunch broccoli

1 garlic clove, minced
1/4 lb. mushrooms, sliced
1/2 teaspoon dried red-pepper flakes
Salt
Freshly ground black pepper

In a large saucepan, bring 3 to 4 quarts water to a boil. Add 1/4 teaspoon oil and pasta; cook according to package directions until tender but firm to the bite. While pasta cooks, combine ricotta and Parmesan cheeses; set aside. Break cauliflower and broccoli into flowerets, reserving stems for other use. Place cauliflower and broccoli flowerets on a rack in a wok over simmering water; cover and steam 5 minutes or until crisp-tender; set aside. Drain water from wok; place over high heat. When dry, add remaining 2 teaspoons oil. When hot, add garlic and mushrooms; stir-fry 1 minute. Add red-pepper flakes; season to taste with salt and black pepper. Reduce heat to medium. Add cauliflower and broccoli flowerets; stir-fry until heated through. Drain cooked pasta. Stir pasta and cheese mixture into vegetable mixture until heated through. Makes 4 servings.

About 340 calories per serving.

Mezzani with Fresh Tomatoes

Mezzani, *an elbow macaroni, made special with fresh tomatoes and herbs.*

1/4 teaspoon peanut oil or vegetable oil
1 (8-oz.) pkg. mezzani or elbow macaroni
4 large tomatoes
1/4 teaspoon dried leaf oregano

1/4 teaspoon dried red-pepper flakes
1 tablespoon capers, drained
1 tablespoon minced fresh parsley

In a large saucepan, bring 3 to 4 quarts water to a boil. Add oil and mezzani or macaroni; cook according to package directions until tender but firm to the bite. While pasta cooks, bring a small saucepan of water to a boil. Plunge each tomato into boiling water 10 to 15 seconds. Hold each tomato under cold running water and peel off skin. Remove and discard cores. Cut tomatoes into large chunks, reserving juice. Place wok over high heat; add oregano, red-pepper flakes, capers and tomatoes with juice. Stir-fry tomatoes, breaking them up until reduced to a thick chunky sauce. Drain cooked pasta; add pasta and parsley to hot sauce. Toss briefly to blend. Serve immediately. Makes 4 servings.

About 230 calories per serving.

How to Make Beef & Zucchini with Pasta

1/Cut zucchini lengthwise in thin slices; stack slices and cut in lengthwise julienne strips.

2/Drain cooked pasta; stir pasta and cheese into wok. Stir-fry until hot.

Beef & Zucchini with Pasta

A delicious combination of flavors.

4 oz. linguine
2-1/8 teaspoons peanut oil or vegetable oil
3 to 4 small zucchini, about 1 lb.
1 small garlic clove, crushed
1/2 lb. lean ground beef
1 (16-oz.) can whole peeled tomatoes,
  slightly chopped

1/4 cup packed chopped fresh basil or
  1 tablespoon dried leaf basil
1/8 teaspoon dried leaf thyme
1/8 teaspoon dried leaf oregano
1/2 teaspoon salt
1/8 teaspoon freshly ground black pepper
1 tablespoon grated Parmesan cheese

Break linguine into 2-inch pieces. In a large saucepan, bring 3 to 4 quarts water to a boil. Add 1/8 teaspoon oil and linguine; cook according to package directions until tender but firm to the bite. While pasta cooks, cut zucchini lengthwise in thin slices; stack slices and cut in lengthwise julienne strips. Place wok over high heat; add remaining 2 teaspoons oil. When hot, add garlic; stir-fry until lightly browned. Remove and discard garlic. Add ground beef to wok; stir-fry, breaking up meat, until lightly browned. Stir in zucchini strips; stir-fry 1 minute. Add tomatoes with juice, basil, thyme, oregano, salt and pepper. Drain cooked pasta; stir cooked pasta and cheese into wok. Stir-fry until mixture it bubbly hot. Makes 4 servings.

About 170 calories per serving.

Linguine with Mushroom Sauce

A perfect mushroom sauce to serve over any pasta.

1-1/4 teaspoons peanut oil or
    vegetable oil
1 (8-oz.) pkg. linguine or
    other thin pasta
1/2 lb. mushrooms, coarsely chopped
1/4 cup chopped shallots
1/2 teaspoon salt

Freshly ground black pepper
2 tablespoons dry white wine
1 cup Vegetable Broth or Chicken Broth,
    pages 152-153, canned broth or water
1 teaspoon cornstarch
2 teaspoons grated Parmesan cheese

In a large saucepan, bring 3 to 4 quarts water to a boil. Add 1/4 teaspoon oil and pasta; cook according to package directions until tender but firm to the bite. While pasta cooks, prepare sauce. Place wok over medium-high heat; add remaining 1 teaspoon oil. When hot, add mushrooms and shallots; stir-fry 1 minute. Cover and steam until mushrooms give off some liquid. Season to taste with salt and pepper. Add wine and 3/4 cup broth or water. Bring to a boil; boil 2 minutes. Stir cornstarch into remaining 1/4 cup broth. When smooth, stir into simmering sauce; stir until sauce slightly thickens. To serve, drain cooked pasta; place in a serving dish. Top with hot mushroom sauce; sprinkle with cheese. Makes 4 servings.

About 270 calories per serving.

Cajun Rice

If you love the foods of New Orleans, try this richly flavored rice dish.

1/2 lb. chicken livers
2 tablespoons peanut oil or vegetable oil
Salt
Freshly ground black pepper
1 large onion, chopped

1 tablespoon water
About 1/2 teaspoon ground sage
1 teaspoon sugar
1 tablespoon brandy
2 cups cold cooked rice

Clean chicken livers, removing any large veins; cut into quarters. Place wok over high heat; add 1 tablespoon oil. When hot, add livers; stir-fry 1 to 2 minutes. Season with salt and pepper. Drain on paper towels; set aside. Wipe wok clean; place over medium heat. Add onion; stir-fry 30 seconds. Sprinkle with water; cover and steam 1 minute. Stir-fry until crisp-tender. Increase heat to high. When hot, stir in remaining 1 tablespoon oil and livers. Sprinkle with sage and sugar; stir until heated through. Add brandy; cover and steam until brandy has evaporated. Add rice; stir until heated through. Serve immediately. Makes 4 servings.

About 240 calories per serving.

Stir-Fried Rice with Pork

A great recipe to use cold leftover rice.

1/2 lb. lean boneless pork
1 tablespoon Madeira
1 teaspoon sesame oil
1 teaspoon cornstarch
4 teaspoons peanut oil or vegetable oil
1 onion, chopped
1 small green bell pepper, cut in thin strips

1 garlic clove, crushed
1/4 cup Vegetable Broth or Chicken Broth,
    pages 152-153, canned broth or water
2 cups cold cooked rice
1 egg, lightly beaten
About 3 tablespoons soy sauce

Cut pork into 1/2-inch cubes. In a small bowl, combine pork, Madeira, sesame oil and cornstarch; stir to blend. Cover and let stand 20 minutes. Place wok over medium heat; add 2 teaspoons peanut oil or vegetable oil. When hot, add onion and bell pepper; stir-fry 1 minute or until crisp-tender. Remove from wok; set aside. Wipe wok clean; add remaining 2 teaspoons oil. When hot, add garlic; stir-fry until lightly browned. Remove and discard garlic. Add marinated pork pieces with marinade and broth or water. Cover and steam 1 minute. Uncover and stir-fry until liquid evaporates. Add onion and bell pepper; stir-fry 30 seconds. Add rice; toss and stir until heated through. Add egg; stir until cooked and mixture is thoroughly combined. Season to taste with soy sauce. Makes 4 servings.

About 260 calories per serving.

Lemon-Thyme Rice with Pork

Fresh lemon juice gives this an especially good flavor.

2 teaspoons peanut oil or vegetable oil
1 small onion, chopped
1-1/2 teaspoons grated lemon peel
1 teaspoon dried leaf thyme, crushed
1 cup basmati rice or long-grain rice

2 cups Chicken Broth, page 153,
    canned broth or water
1 teaspoon fresh lemon juice
1/8 teaspoon salt
1 cup diced cooked pork

Place wok over high heat; add oil. When hot, add onion; stir-fry until crisp-tender. Stir in lemon peel and thyme; stir-fry 30 seconds. Add rice, broth or water, and lemon juice; bring to a boil. Reduce heat; cover and simmer 20 minutes or until rice is tender and almost all liquid is absorbed. Stir in salt and pork. Remove from heat; cover and let stand 2 minutes or until liquid is absorbed and pork is heated through. Fluff with a fork immediately before serving. Makes 4 servings.

About 310 calories per serving.

Latin-Style Rice with Beef

Raisins and Madeira add an interesting sweetness to this dish.

1/4 cup raisins
2 tablespoons Madeira
2 teaspoons peanut oil or vegetable oil
1 garlic clove, crushed
1 large green bell pepper, chopped
1 large onion, chopped
1 tablespoon water

1/2 lb. lean ground beef
1/4 cup Vegetable Broth or Chicken Broth,
   pages 152-153, or canned broth
2 tablespoons chopped green olives
2 cups cold cooked rice

In a small bowl, soak raisins in Madeira 30 minutes. Place wok over high heat; add oil. When hot, add garlic; stir until lightly browned. Remove and discard garlic. Add bell pepper and onion; stir-fry 1 minute. Sprinkle with 1 tablespoon water; cover and steam about 1 minute. Stir in beef; cook, stirring frequently, until no longer pink. Add raisins, Madeira and broth; cook, stirring frequently, until liquid evaporates. Stir in olives and rice; stir-fry until heated through. Makes 4 servings.

About 260 calories per serving.

Pilaf with Beef

Flavorful basmati rice is the perfect choice for a light and fluffy pilaf.

2 teaspoons peanut oil or vegetable oil
2 small garlic cloves, minced
1 teaspoon Quatre Epices, page 155
1 cup basmati rice or long-grain rice

2 cups Beef Broth, page 152, canned broth
   or water
1/2 teaspoon salt
1 cup diced cooked beef

Place wok over high heat; add oil. When hot, stir in garlic, spices and rice; stir-fry 30 seconds. Add broth or water; bring to a boil. Reduce heat; cover and simmer 20 minutes or until rice is tender and almost all liquid is absorbed. Stir in salt and beef. Remove from heat; cover and let stand 2 minutes or until liquid is absorbed and beef is heated through. Fluff with a fork immediately before serving. Makes 4 servings.

About 270 calories per serving.

Basmati rice, grown in the Himalayas, gives off a delightful pecan aroma during cooking.

Stir-Fried Rice with Seafood

For variety, use other seafood in this delicious stir-fry.

Water
1 tablespoon tomato paste
2 teaspoons peanut oil or vegetable oil
1 small onion, minced
1 green bell pepper, minced
1/4 lb. mushrooms, minced
2 large tomatoes, peeled, seeded,
   cut in 1/4-inch cubes

1 teaspoon sugar
1/2 teaspoon paprika
1/2 teaspoon cumin seed
1 cup shucked, drained oysters
1/2 lb. raw shrimp, peeled, deveined
2 cups cold cooked rice
Salt
Freshly ground black pepper

In a small bowl, combine 1/2 cup water and tomato paste; set aside. Place wok over low heat; add oil. When hot, add onion, bell pepper and mushrooms; stir-fry 1 minute. Sprinkle with 1 tablespoon water; cover and steam 1 minute. Increase heat to high; add tomatoes. Stir-fry until heated through. Stir in tomato-paste mixture, sugar, paprika, cumin, oysters and shrimp; stir-fry until shrimp turn pink and oyster edges begin to curl. Stir in rice; season to taste with salt and black pepper. Stir-fry until heated through. Serve immediately. Makes 4 servings.

About 280 calories per serving.

Steamed Rice with Clams

Prepare ahead; then at serving time, reheat and stir in clams.

2 pints shucked fresh clams in juice
Water
1 teaspoon peanut oil or vegetable oil
1 small onion, finely chopped
1/4 lb. mushrooms, sliced
1 garlic clove, minced
1 teaspoon turmeric

1/2 teaspoon dried leaf oregano, crushed
1 (16-oz.) can peeled tomatoes
1/4 teaspoon dried red-pepper flakes
1/4 teaspoon salt
1/8 teaspoon freshly ground black pepper
1-1/2 cups long-grain rice
1/4 cup minced fresh parsley

Drain clam juice into a 4-cup measure; add enough water to make 2-3/4 cups liquid. Chop clams; set aside. Place wok over high heat; add oil. When hot, add onion and mushrooms; stir-fry 1 minute. Cover and steam 30 seconds. Stir in garlic; stir-fry until mushrooms give off some liquid. Stir in turmeric and oregano. Crush tomatoes; add tomatoes and juice to wok. Season with red-pepper flakes, salt and black pepper. Add clam juice and water; bring to a simmer. Stir in rice; cover and simmer 20 minutes or until rice is tender and almost all liquid has been absorbed. Stir in clams until heated through. Serve hot, garnished with parsley. Makes 4 servings.

About 360 calories per serving.

How to Make Saffron Rice with Shrimp

1/Add cooked shrimp and bell-pepper strips to saffron rice mixture. Toss lightly to blend.

2/Fluff rice mixture with a fork immediately before serving.

Saffron Rice with Shrimp

Saffron, the world's most expensive spice, is the orange stigma of a flowering crocus.

2 teaspoons peanut oil or vegetable oil
1 small red or green bell pepper,
  cut in thin strips
1 small onion, chopped
1 cup basmati rice or long-grain rice
1/2 teaspoon saffron threads, crushed,
  or a pinch of turmeric

2 cups Vegetable Broth or Chicken Broth,
  pages 152-153, canned broth or water
Salt
Freshly ground black pepper
1/2 lb. cooked medium shrimp,
  peeled, deveined

Place wok over high heat; add oil. When hot, add bell pepper; stir-fry 1 minute or until crisp-tender. Remove strips to a small bowl. Add onion to wok; stir-fry 1 minute or until crisp-tender. Stir in rice and saffron or turmeric; stir-fry 30 seconds. Add broth or water; bring to a boil. Reduce heat; cover and simmer 20 minutes or until rice is tender and almost all liquid is absorbed. Season to taste with salt and black pepper. With a fork, stir in bell pepper and shrimp. Remove from heat; cover and let stand 2 minutes or until liquid is absorbed and shrimp are heated through. Fluff with a fork immediately before serving. Makes 4 servings.

About 280 calories per serving.

Hawaiian Rice

Such a beautiful dish; the star attraction on your next buffet table.

1/4 lb. mushrooms, sliced
1 small green bell pepper, diced
1 small red bell pepper, diced
1 onion, diced
1 (8-oz.) can pineapple chunks in
    unsweetened juice
2 tablespoons chopped fresh basil or
    2 teaspoons dried leaf basil

1/4 teaspoon ground ginger
3 oz. lean cooked ham, cut in cubes
1/2 cup diced water chestnuts
2 cups cold cooked rice
Salt
Freshly ground black pepper

Place wok over medium heat. When hot, add mushrooms, bell peppers and onion; stir-fry 1 minute. Drain juice from pineapple, reserving pineapple; sprinkle about 2 tablespoons juice over hot vegetables. Reserve remaining juice for another use. Cover and steam until mushrooms give off some liquid. Increase heat to high; add basil, ginger, ham, pineapple chunks and water chestnuts; stir-fry 30 seconds. Stir in rice, lifting and tossing until ingredients are hot. Season to taste with salt and black pepper. Makes 4 servings.

About 180 calories per serving.

Curried Rice with Chicken

The flavor of India, the spice of any diet.

2 teaspoons peanut oil or vegetable oil
6 shallots, chopped
About 2 teaspoons curry powder
1 cup basmati rice or long-grain rice
1-1/2 cups Chicken Broth or Vegetable Broth,
    pages 152-153, canned broth or water

1/2 cup tomato juice
1/2 teaspoon salt
1/8 teaspoon freshly ground black pepper
1 cup diced, cooked skinned chicken breast

Place wok over high heat; add oil. When hot, add shallots; stir-fry until crisp-tender. Stir in curry powder to taste; stir 30 seconds or until fragrant. Add rice, broth or water, and tomato juice. Bring to a boil; reduce heat. Cover and simmer 20 minutes or until rice is tender and almost all liquid is absorbed. Stir in salt, pepper and chicken. Remove from heat; cover and let stand 2 minutes or until liquid is absorbed and chicken is heated through. Fluff with a fork immediately before serving. Makes 4 servings.

About 280 calories per serving.

Hawaiian Rice

Stir-Fried Rice with Turkey

Ground turkey is a delightful meaty surprise.

1/2 lb. ground raw turkey, thawed if frozen	1 to 2 tablespoons water
About 3 tablespoons soy sauce	2 tablespoons Madeira
2 teaspoons peanut oil or vegetable oil	1/2 cup fresh or thawed frozen green peas
1 garlic clove, crushed	3 cups cold cooked rice
4 canned water chestnuts, coarsely chopped	1 egg, lightly beaten

In a medium bowl, combine turkey and 2 tablespoons soy sauce. Place wok over high heat; add oil. When hot, add garlic; stir until lightly browned. Remove and discard garlic. Add seasoned turkey and water chestnuts; stir-fry 1 minute, adding a little water, if necessary, to keep mixture from sticking. Pour in remaining water and Madeira. Cover and steam 1 minute. Uncover and stir-fry until liquid has evaporated. Add peas and rice, tossing and stirring until heated through. Add egg; stir until cooked and mixture is thoroughly combined. Season to taste with soy sauce. Makes 4 servings.

About 260 calories per serving.

Rice Provençal with Turkey or Veal

The herb mixture used in this recipe is typical of Southern France.

2 teaspoons peanut oil or vegetable oil	2 cups Chicken Broth or Vegetable Broth,
1 small red onion, chopped	pages 152-153, canned broth or water
1 small garlic clove, minced	1/8 teaspoon salt
1 tablespoon herbs of Provence	1 cup diced cooked turkey breast or veal
1 cup basmati rice or long-grain rice	

Place wok over high heat; add oil. When hot, add onion; stir-fry until crisp-tender. Stir in garlic, herbs and rice. Add broth or water; bring to a boil. Reduce heat; cover and simmer 20 minutes or until tender and almost all liquid is absorbed. Stir in salt and turkey or veal. Remove from heat; cover and let stand 2 minutes or until liquid is absorbed and meat is heated through. Fluff with a fork immediately before serving. Makes 4 servings.

About 280 calories per serving.

Herbs of Provence is a blend of marjoram, thyme, summer savory, sweet basil, rosemary, sage, fennel seed and lavender.

Stir-Fried Rice with Vegetables

A hearty diet meal that tastes wonderful.

1 teaspoon peanut oil or vegetable oil
1/4 lb. mushrooms, coarsely chopped
1 large onion, chopped
1 green bell pepper, chopped
1/4 lb. young green beans
1 small garlic clove, minced

1 (16-oz.) can Italian-style peeled
  tomatoes with basil
1 teaspoon dried leaf oregano
1/4 teaspoon salt
1/2 cup canned or frozen whole-kernel corn
3 cups cold cooked rice

Place wok over high heat; add oil. When hot, add mushrooms, onion, green pepper and green beans; stir-fry 1 minute. Cover and steam 1 minute; add garlic. Crush tomatoes; add to wok along with juice, oregano and salt. Bring to a boil; boil until reduced by about 1/2. Stir in corn and rice. Stir-fry until heated through. Makes 4 servings.

About 210 calories per serving.

Creole Red Beans & Rice

You won't feel deprived with this hearty lunch or supper dish.

1 teaspoon peanut oil or vegetable oil
1 large onion, chopped
1 small green bell pepper, chopped
1 garlic clove, minced
1 (16-oz.) can peeled tomatoes
1 tablespoon tomato paste
1 teaspoon Quatre Epices, page 155

1/8 teaspoon salt
2 cups cold cooked rice
1 cup cooked, drained red kidney beans
1 cup packed shredded romaine or
  iceberg lettuce
1/2 cup shredded Monterey Jack or
  brick cheese (2 oz.)

Lightly oil bottom and side of wok; place over high heat. When hot, add onion and bell pepper; stir-fry about 1 minute. Add garlic; stir-fry 30 seconds. Add tomatoes with juice, tomato paste, Quatre Epices and salt. Stir, breaking up tomatoes with spoon. Reduce heat and simmer, *stirring occasionally,* about 5 minutes. Stir in rice and beans; cook, stirring until heated through. Remove wok from heat; stir in romaine or lettuce. Serve hot, garnished with cheese. Makes 4 servings.

About 350 calories per serving.

DESSERTS

Even if you are on a restricted diet, you don't have to go without dessert. In this chapter, you will find excellent dessert recipes, all 200 calories or less. You don't have to serve low-calorie, diet-minded entrees to serve these desserts. They can be served with any meal.

These desserts are quick to prepare. Some, like the custard desserts, require chilling, and, of course, the cakes must be made ahead so they have time to cool.

Desserts are included to fit every occasion and every mood. Bananas Anisette are perfect for an elegant little dinner party, while Apple-Spice Pudding Cake is fun to have on hand after a casual get together, al fresco-type meal. The Meringue Soufflé is so festive, so delicious, it may well become your own specialty of the house, especially during the holiday season. It's delicious to serve to dieters and non-dieters alike.

Menu

Breakfast
1/2 cup skim milk   1 oz. shredded wheat
1/2 cup blueberries
1 bran muffin
Coffee or tea
Snack
1/2 cup low-fat yogurt
Lunch
Huevos Rancheros, page 70
1 corn muffin
Dinner
2 Tabbouleh-Stuffed Mushrooms, page 26
Indian Keema with Peas, page 68
Blueberry-Apricot Dessert, page 137
3 oz. dry white wine
Snack
1 apple

About 1200 calories

Pears in Buttery-Rum Chocolate Sauce

For dieter's, this is a fantasy come true.

4 Anjou pears or other pears
2 teaspoons fresh lemon juice
2 teaspoons butter-flavored granules
1/2 cup hot water
1 (1.5-oz.) pkg. sugar-free chocolate
  pudding mix

2 tablespoons instant non-fat milk powder
1 cup cold water
1 tablespoon light rum or rum flavoring
4 teaspoons sugar-free
  strawberry-flavored gelatin powder

Cut a thin slice from bottom of each pear. With a small knife or apple corer, remove seeds and core from cut end of each pear. Place pears, stem-side up, in a shallow steaming dish. Place dish on a rack in a wok over simmering water; cover and steam 5 to 15 minutes or until tender. Cooking time will depend on ripeness of pears. Remove from wok; cool to room temperature. Hold each pear under cold running water and peel off skin. Rub each pear with lemon juice. In a small bowl, dissolve butter granules in 1/2 cup hot water; cool to room temperature. In a medium bowl, combine pudding mix and milk powder; beat in cold water until smooth. Stir in cooled butter mixture and rum or rum flavoring. Pour into 4 shallow dessert dishes. Sprinkle each pear lightly with 1 teaspoon gelatin powder. Place pears in center of dessert dishes, pressing down lightly to set firmly in pudding mixture. Refrigerate until chilled. Makes 4 servings.

About 190 calories per serving.

Pears in Raspberry Glaze

A truly beautiful dessert.

1/4 cup fresh lemon juice
Water
3 large ripe Anjou pears
2 tablespoons orange juice or
  orange liqueur

1/2 (3-oz) pkg. sugar-free
  raspberry-flavored gelatin powder

In a large bowl, combine lemon juice and 3 cups water. Cut each pear, from stem to bottom, into 4 wedges; remove and discard peel and core. Cut pears into bite-sized cubes; drop into lemon juice to prevent discoloration. Drain pear cubes; place in an 8-inch-square baking dish or round 8-inch baking dish. Dissolve gelatin in 1-1/2 cups cold water and juice or liqueur. Pour mixture over pear cubes; gently stir and toss pears to coat evenly with mixture. Place dish on a rack in a wok over simmering water. Cover and steam 10 minutes or until pears can be easily pierced. Remove dish from wok; let pears and liquid cool to room temperature, basting frequently. Refrigerate until chilled, basting occasionally. Liquid will thicken. Stir with a fork or spoon to blend. Spoon into shallow dessert dishes. Makes 4 servings.

About 170 calories per serving.

Stir-Fried Peaches in Brandy

Prepare this elegant dessert when peaches are at the peak of the season.

3 peaches
1 tablespoon brandy

1/4 teaspoon ground ginger
1 teaspoon brown sugar

Bring a small pan of water to a boil. Plunge each peach into boiling water 30 seconds; then hold under cold running water and slip off skin. Cut each peach in 1/2, removing pits. Cut peaches into thick slices. Place wok over high heat. When hot, add peach slices. Using a spatula, stir-fry 2 to 3 minutes, lifting slices and flipping them against the side of the wok until slightly softened and hot. Add brandy; bring to a boil. Sprinkle with ginger and brown sugar. Stir-fry 30 seconds. Makes 4 servings.

Variation
Stir-Fried Peaches are also excellent over thin slices of Lemony Low-Calorie Sponge Cake, page 147, or topped with frozen ice milk.

About 40 calories per serving.

Poached Peaches with Cheese Filling

Prepare these peaches ahead, then serve chilled as a special ending to any meal.

2 large peaches
3 tablespoons orange juice or orange liqueur

4 oz. Neufchâtel cheese, room temperature
1 oz. toasted slivered almonds

For poached peaches, bring a small pan of water to a boil. Plunge each peach into boiling water 30 seconds; then hold under cold running water and slip off skin. Cut each peach in 1/2, removing pits. Place peach halves, cut-side up, in an 8-inch-square baking dish. Spoon 2 tablespoons juice or liqueur over peach halves. Place dish on a rack in a wok over simmering water. Cover and steam 5 to 10 minutes or until peach halves can be easily pierced. Remove dish from wok; cool slightly. Refrigerate until chilled.
For filling, in a small bowl, beat together cheese and remaining 1 tablespoon juice or liqueur until light and fluffy. Refrigerate until chilled.
To serve, place each peach half on a small plate; fill with cheese mixture. Garnish with almonds. Makes 4 servings.

About 140 calories per serving.

Blueberry-Apricot Dessert

This heavenly dessert uses non-alcoholic cassis or black-currant syrup.

2 small shortbread cookies
1 pint fresh blueberries
2 tablespoons black-currant syrup

4 fresh apricots
Vanilla-Yogurt Sauce, page 138, if desired

In a food processor fitted with a metal blade, crush cookies to crumbs. Rinse and dry blueberries; place in an 8-inch-square baking dish; stir in crumbs and syrup. Cut apricots in 1/2; place, cut-side down, over blueberry mixture. Place dish on a rack in a wok over simmering water. Cover and steam 10 to 15 minutes or until apricots can be easily pierced. Serve warm or cold with Vanilla-Yogurt Sauce, if desired. Makes 4 servings.

About 100 calories per serving.

Honey-Graham Cake

Light and airy like a sponge cake, but with the dense flavor of honey and graham-cracker crumbs.

Cake:
5 eggs, separated
3/4 cup sugar
1/4 cup honey
1/4 cup orange juice

1 tablespoon fresh lemon juice
1 tablespoon grated lemon peel
1/2 cup graham-cracker crumbs
1/2 cup sifted all-purpose flour

Orange-Honey Yogurt Sauce:
1 (8-oz.) carton plain low-fat yogurt
1 tablespoon thawed frozen orange-juice
  concentrate

1 tablespoon honey

For sauce, in a small bowl, stir together yogurt, orange-juice concentrate and honey; beat until blended. Cover and refrigerate until ready to serve.
For cake, generously butter a 9-inch-square baking pan. In a large bowl, beat egg yolks 3 to 4 minutes or until thick and lemon colored. Add sugar, 1/4 cup at a time, beating well after each addition. Beat in honey, orange juice, lemon juice and lemon peel. Fold in graham-cracker crumbs and flour. In a medium bowl, beat egg whites until stiff peaks form. Gently fold beaten egg whites into batter. Pour into buttered pan. Place on a rack in a wok over simmering water. Cover and steam 20 to 25 minutes or until a wooden pick inserted in center of cake comes out clean. Cool on a rack 10 to 15 minutes. Then loosen edges and turn out onto rack; cool completely. Cut into 9 (3-inch) squares. Serve with Orange-Honey Yogurt Sauce. Makes 9 servings.

About 200 calories per serving.

Golden Apples

These apples glisten with gold.

**4 large Golden Delicious, Granny Smith
  or Pippin apples**
1/2 small lemon
1/2 cup water
1 teaspoon liquid sugar substitute

3 tablespoons low-sugar orange marmalade
**1 (3-oz.) pkg. sugar-free orange-flavored
  gelatin**

Vanilla-Yogurt Sauce:
1/2 cup plain low-fat yogurt
1/4 teaspoon vanilla extract

1/2 teaspoon liquid sugar substitute

Peel top third of each apple, reserving peelings. Remove apple cores. Rub peeled portion of each apple with cut side of lemon; squeeze lemon half, then remove lemon peel and finely chop. Pour water in an 8-inch-square baking dish. Stir in lemon juice and sugar substitute. Add apple peelings and lemon peel. Fill each apple with about 2 teaspoons marmalade; arrange in baking dish. Reserve 1/2 the gelatin powder; sprinkle remaining gelatin evenly over peeled portion of apples. Place dish on a rack in a wok over simmering water. Cover and steam 25 to 30 minutes or until apples are tender. Remove dish from wok; immediately sprinkle remaining gelatin over each apple. Cool apples in syrup.

For sauce, in a small bowl, combine ingredients; blend well. Refrigerate until chilled.

To complete, serve apples warm or at room temperature. Top each apple with sauce, if desired. Makes 4 servings.

About 200 calories per serving.

How to Make Golden Apples

1/Peel top third of each apple; remove cores. Rub peeled portion of each apple with cut side of a lemon.

2/Arrange apples in baking dish; fill each apple with about 2 teaspoons marmalade.

Apples with Honey-Cheese Sauce

A delightful way to enjoy an all-American favorite — apples.

1/4 cup low-fat ricotta cheese	**4 cooking apples**
2 tablespoons plain low-fat yogurt	**1 tablespoon brandy**
2 teaspoons honey	**1 tablespoon toasted slivered almonds**
1/4 teaspoon vanilla extract	

In a blender or food processor fitted with a metal blade, combine cheese, yogurt, honey and vanilla; process until smooth. Spoon into a medium bowl. Cover and refrigerate 1 hour. Peel, core and dice apples. Place wok over high heat. When hot, add apples; stir-fry 1 minute or until apples begin to soften. Add brandy; boil until evaporated, stirring occasionally. Spoon apples into 4 shallow dessert dishes. Top with chilled cheese sauce; garnish with almonds. Makes 4 servings.

About 130 calories per serving.

Pineapple Puffs

Light, beautiful and especially delicious—a wonderful way to end a meal.

1 (8-oz.) can pineapple slices in unsweetened juice	**4 teaspoons light rum**
1 teaspoon finely grated lemon peel	**1 egg white**
	1/8 teaspoon cream of tartar
4 teaspoons light-brown sugar	**1/4 cup plus 2 teaspoons granulated sugar**

Drain pineapple, reserving juice. Place 4 slices, in a single layer, in a shallow steamer dish. Reserve other slices for other use. In a small saucepan over low heat, combine pineapple juice and lemon peel; simmer 5 minutes. Pour hot juice around pineapple slices in steamer dish. Sprinkle each slice with 1 teaspoon brown sugar and 1 teaspoon rum. In a small bowl, beat egg white with cream of tartar until frothy; gradually beat in 1/4 cup granulated sugar until reaching a stiff and glossy meringue. Spoon 1/4 of meringue over each pineapple slice; sprinkle with remaining 2 teaspoons granulated sugar. Place dish on a rack in a wok over simmering water. Cover and steam 5 to 6 minutes or until meringues are firm to the touch. Remove from wok; cool on a rack. Using a spatula, transfer each puff to a dessert dish. Pour juice around puffs. Garnish as desired. Makes 4 servings.

About 120 calories per serving.

Carrot-Raisin Pudding

Simply delicious, and good for you, too.

6 to 8 carrots, about 2 lbs., thinly sliced	**1/4 teaspoon ground cinnamon**
1/2 cup water	**1/8 teaspoon ground nutmeg**
1/2 orange juice	**1/8 teaspoon ground ginger**
1/8 teaspoon salt	**1/2 cup raisins**
1/2 cup sugar	**1/2 cup Vanilla-Yogurt Sauce,**
2 eggs	**page 138, if desired**

Butter a 1-1/2-quart soufflé dish or deep steaming dish. In a small saucepan, combine carrots and water; cook over medium heat until tender. In a blender or food processor fitted with a metal blade, puree cooked carrots, any remaining cooking liquid and orange juice. Blend in salt, sugar, eggs, cinnamon, nutmeg and ginger. Stir in raisins. Spoon mixture into buttered dish. Place dish on a rack in a wok over simmering water; cover and steam 25 to 30 minutes or until firm and a knife inserted off-center comes out clean. Refrigerate until chilled. Spoon into dessert dishes; top each serving with 1 tablespoon Vanilla-Yogurt Sauce, if desired. Makes 8 servings.

About 150 calories per serving.

Meringue Soufflé with Strawberry Sauce

A fluffy cloud — a light and airy dessert.

Soufflé:

2 teaspoons sugar

6 large egg whites

1/4 teaspoon cream of tartar

3/4 cup sugar

1 teaspoon vanilla extract

Strawberry Sauce:

1 pint strawberries

1 tablespoon sugar

1 teaspoon grated orange peel or lemon peel

For soufflé, butter a 2-quart soufflé dish or straight-sided casserole. Sprinkle with 2 teaspoons sugar, tipping dish to distribute sugar evenly. In a large bowl, beat egg whites until frothy. Gradually beat in cream of tartar; beat until soft peaks form. Add 3/4 cup sugar, 1 tablespoon at a time, beating well after each addition. Fold in vanilla. Spoon into prepared dish. Place dish on a rack in a wok over simmering water. Cover with a high domed lid and steam 25 to 30 minutes or until top feels dry when gently touched. Transfer dish to a cooling rack; cool 5 minutes. Soufflé will shrink about 1 inch. Invert soufflé onto a serving plate. Cool to room temperature.

For sauce, clean strawberries. Place 1/2 the berries in a medium bowl; mash to a chunky sauce. Stir in sugar; let stand 10 minutes or until sugar dissolves. Coarsely chop remaining berries; add to sauce. Stir in grated orange peel or lemon peel.

To complete, cut soufflé into thick wedges; arrange slices on dessert plates. Spoon sauce over each serving. Makes 4 servings.

About 200 calories per serving.

How to Make Meringue Soufflé with Sauce

1/Cover and steam soufflé 25 to 30 minutes or until top feels dry when gently touched.

2/Cut soufflé into wedges; arrange on dessert plates. Spoon sauce over each serving.

Pumpkin Meringue Pudding

Don't miss out on the holiday desserts; enjoy this low-calorie pudding.

1 teaspoon butter
1/4 cup graham-cracker crumbs
3 eggs, 2 separated
1 (16-oz.) can solid-pack pumpkin
Liquid sugar substitute to equal
   1/4 cup sugar
1/4 teaspoon salt
1-1/4 teaspoons ground cinnamon

1/2 teaspoon ground ginger
1/4 teaspoon ground cloves
6 tablespoons instant non-fat milk powder
3/4 cup plus 1 tablespoon water
1/2 teaspoon rum flavoring or
   vanilla extract
1/8 teaspoon cream of tartar
1/4 cup plus 1 tablespoon sugar

Place butter in an 8-inch-square baking dish; place on a rack in a wok over simmering water. Cover and steam 30 seconds until melted; swirl to distribute evenly. Sprinkle with crumbs; press into butter. In a large bowl, beat 1 egg and 2 egg yolks. Stir in pumpkin, sugar substitute, salt, 1 teaspoon cinnamon, ginger and cloves. Stir in milk powder, water and rum flavoring or vanilla. Pour into prepared dish; place on a rack in a wok over simmering water. Cover and steam 30 to 35 minutes or until a knife inserted off-center comes out clean. In a medium bowl, beat 2 egg whites with cream of tartar until frothy; gradually beat in 1/4 cup sugar until whites reach a stiff glossy meringue. Top pudding with meringue; sprinkle with remaining sugar and cinnamon. Cover and steam 5 minutes or until meringue is firm; cool. Makes 6 servings.

About 160 calories per serving.

Espresso Custard with Lemon Topping

A very light and airy custard.

Custard:
2 large eggs
1-1/2 teaspoons instant espresso
  coffee powder
5 tablespoons instant non-fat milk powder

1/4 cup sugar
1 cup water
1/2 teaspoon vanilla extract

Fluffy Lemon Topping:
1 (8-oz.) carton plain low-fat yogurt
1/2 (1.25-oz.) pkg. sugar-free presweetened
  lemonade-flavored drink mix

For custard, in a medium bowl, beat eggs until light and lemon colored; beat in 1 teaspoon coffee powder, milk powder and sugar. Gradually add water and vanilla, beating as added until smooth. Place 4 individual soufflé dishes or 4 (1-cup) custard cups in an 8-inch-square baking dish. Ladle custard mixture into each dish. Carefully pour boiling water into baking dish around custard, bringing water about 1/2 way up dishes. Fill a wok with water to about 1-inch over steamer rack; bring to a simmer. Place dish of custards on a rack in wok; cover and cook until a knife inserted off-center in custard comes out clean. Remove dish from wok; transfer custard cups to a cooling rack. Cool slightly; then cover and refrigerate until chilled.

For topping, in a medium bowl, combine yogurt and drink mix; stir until smooth. Cover and refrigerate until chilled.

To serve, top each custard with a dollop of topping. Sprinkle each lightly with remaining 1/2 teaspoon espresso coffee powder. Makes 4 servings.

About 180 calories per serving.

Tropical Cheesecake with Fruit Topping

This sweet indulgence is a calorie-affordable cheesecake.

Cheesecake:

1 teaspoon butter
1/2 cup graham-cracker crumbs
1-3/4 cups low-fat cottage cheese
1/4 cup low-fat ricotta cheese
1 (0.41-oz.) pkg. sugar-free presweetened
   tropical-flavored drink mix

5 tablespoons instant non-fat milk powder
3/4 cup water
3 eggs

Strawberry Glaze with Fresh Fruit:

1 (0.3-oz.) pkg. sugar-free
   strawberry-flavored gelatin
1 cup boiling water
1/2 cup cold water

1 cup coarsely chopped strawberries
1/2 banana, sliced
1/2 cup pineapple chunks in unsweetened juice,
   drained

For cheesecake, place butter in a 9-inch pie pan. Place pan on a rack in a wok over simmering water. Cover and steam 30 seconds or until butter has melted. Remove from wok; swirl to distribute butter evenly over bottom. Sprinkle evenly with cracker crumbs; press crumbs into butter. In a food processor fitted with a metal blade, combine cottage cheese, ricotta cheese, drink mix, milk powder, water and eggs; process until blended and smooth. Or press cottage cheese and ricotta cheese through a fine sieve or food mill into a medium bowl. Add remaining ingredients as above, beating well after each addition. Pour mixture into crumb-lined pan. Place pan on a rack in a wok over simmering water. Cover and steam 30 to 35 minutes or until top is firm and a knife inserted off-center comes out clean. Add water to wok as needed to maintain level. Refrigerate cheesecake until chilled.

For topping, in a medium bowl, dissolve gelatin in boiling water; add cold water. Refrigerate until thick and syrupy but not set.

To complete, stir fruit into topping. Spoon over cheesecake. Refrigerate until gelatin has set. Makes 8 servings.

About 150 calories per serving.

Very Lemony Cheesecake

A delightful cheesecake—you won't believe it's so low in calories.

2 tablespoons melted butter
1/2 cup plain graham-craker crumbs
8 oz. firm tofu, rinsed, drained,
   blotted dry, crumbled
1 (8-oz.) pkg. Neufchâtel cheese,
   cut in small cubes

2 eggs
1 (1.25-oz.) pkg. sugar-free presweetened
   lemonade-flavored drink mix
1 teaspoon unflavored gelatin powder
1 cup cold water

In an 8-inch pie plate, combine butter and cracker crumbs; press crumbs evenly on bottom and side of plate. Refrigerate until chilled. In a food processor fitted with a metal blade, combine tofu, cheese, eggs and about 3/4 the package of drink mix; process until smooth. Pour mixture over chilled crumb crust. Place pie plate on a rack in a wok over simmering water. Cover and steam 25 to 30 minutes or until filling is set and a knife inserted off-center comes out clean. Cool on a rack 15 minutes; then refrigerate until chilled. In a small saucepan, sprinkle gelatin over cold water; let stand 3 to 5 minutes to soften. Stir over low heat until gelatin has dissolved. Remove from heat; stir in remaining drink mix until dissolved. Refrigerate until mixture is syrupy and slightly thickened. Pour 1/2 the chilled mixture over top of pie. Leave remaining gelatin mixture at room temperature. Refrigerate pie about 30 minutes or until topping is nearly firm. Pour remaining gelatin mixture over pie. Chill until firmly set. Garnish with lemon, if desired. Makes 8 servings.

About 170 calories per serving.

Lemony Low-Calorie Sponge Cake

The tangy lemon flavor comes from the lemon peel.

3/4 cup milk
1-3/4 cups all-purpose flour
1 tablespoon baking powder
5 eggs, room temperature

1-1/4 cups sugar
2 teaspoons grated lemon peel
1 teaspoon fresh lemon juice

In a small saucepan, heat milk until bubbles form around edge of pan. Remove from heat; set aside. Sift flour with baking powder. In a large bowl, beat eggs at high speed until light and lemon-colored. Add sugar, 2 tablespoons at a time, beating after each addition. Beat 10 minutes or until mixture is light. Fold in flour mixture until smooth. Add warm milk, lemon peel and juice. Pour batter into an ungreased 8-inch (8-cup) ring mold. Place mold on a rack in a wok over simmering water. Cover and steam 30 to 35 minutes or until a wooden pick inserted in center comes out clean. Remove from wok; stand center of pan over neck of a bottle or glass. Cool to room temperature. Remove from pan. Serve plain or with a low-calorie fruit sauce. Makes 12 servings.

About 190 calories per serving.

Very Lemony Cheesecake

Grilled Bananas with Rum

Prepare the sauce ahead; then cook bananas immediately before serving.

1/2 cup vanilla low-fat yogurt   **4 bananas**
1/4 cup light rum

In a small bowl, combine yogurt and 1 tablespoon rum. Refrigerate until chilled or ready to use. Place wok over high heat. Cut bananas lengthwise; then cut each 1/2 crosswise. When wok is very hot, add bananas, cut-side down. Cook 30 seconds. Slices will be moist and flecked with brown. Turn and cook other side until bananas are hot through center. Pour in remaining 3 tablespoons rum. Turn banana slices quickly, cooking only a few seconds. Remove wok from heat. Using a spatula, arrange 4 banana pieces on each of 4 small dessert plates. Top each serving with about 2 tablespoons chilled yogurt mixture. Makes 4 servings.

About 180 calories per serving.

Bananas Anisette

Steam-bake this delicious dessert while you enjoy the main course of your meal.

About 2 teaspoons water   **2 tablespoons anisette liqueur**
4 bananas   **Vanilla-Yogurt Sauce, page 138**
2 teaspoons light-brown sugar

Sprinkle an 8-inch-square baking dish with about 2 teaspoons water. Peel bananas; cut each crosswise in 1/2. Arrange halves in a single layer in prepared dish. Sprinkle evenly with brown sugar and liqueur. Place dish on a rack in a wok over simmering water. Cover and steam until sugar dissolves and bananas are heated through. Do not overcook; bananas should remain firm. Serve warm on small dessert plates. Top with sauce or prepared whipped topping. Makes 4 servings.

About 140 calories per serving.

Apple-Spice Pudding Cake

A rich cake, similar to Christmas pudding, makes any day special.

Cake:

4 eggs, separated
2 cups fruit and fiber-type cereal
1/2 cup skim milk
2 tart apples, coarsely grated
1/2 teaspoon ground cinnamon

1/8 teaspoon ground nutmeg
1 teaspoon vanilla extract
1 tablespoon liquid sugar substitute
1-1/2 teaspoons baking powder

Orange & Lemon Sauce, if desired:

1 teaspoon unflavored gelatin powder
2 tablespoons fresh lemon juice

1-1/2 cups orange juice
About 1 tablespoon liquid sugar substitute

For cake, grease an 8-inch-square baking dish. In a large bowl, beat egg yolks until blended; stir in cereal and milk. Stir in apples, cinnamon, nutmeg, vanilla and sugar substitute. Sprinkle batter evenly with baking powder; fold in. In a medium bowl, beat egg whites until soft peaks form; fold into batter. Spoon mixture into greased baking dish. Place dish on a rack in a wok over simmering water. Cover and steam 25 to 30 minutes or until a wooden pick inserted in center of cake comes out clean. Cool 5 minutes, then invert cake onto a cooling rack; let stand until cool.

For sauce, in a small saucepan, combine gelatin and lemon juice; let stand 3 to 5 minutes or until softened. Place over low heat, stirring until gelatin dissolves; remove from heat. Add orange juice and sugar substitute to taste; stir to blend. Spoon into a serving bowl. Cover and refrigerate until chilled and thickened.

To serve, cut cake into 9 (2-1/2-inch) squares. Serve with Orange & Lemon Sauce, if desired. Makes 9 servings.

About 110 calories per serving.

BASICS

One of the most important features of wok cookery is that it is fast. You can prepare a meal, start to finish, using fresh, healthful ingredients, in a matter of minutes. Slow, pre-cooking is never necessary and very little need be prepared ahead.

Two things will decidedly improve the flavor of any wok-cooked dish. Rich, flavorful homemade stock and seasonings you have blended to your own taste are great if you take the time to make them.

As I'm sure you know, any dish depends on the seasonings used and a richly flavored stock, even in small quantities, can make the difference between good and very special. Included here are recipes for stocks that I have used in this book. Along with them are a few seasoning blends I enjoy using in my cooking. Blend them to suit your own taste. These easy extras add the right touch to make a meal even better and make the weight watcher feel special.

Tofu Croutons

Use with salads, stir-fried dishes or soups; also great for a snack.

**8 oz. firm tofu, rinsed,
   drained, blotted dry**
Chinese Five-Spice Powder, page 156

Garlic salt
Szechuan-Peppercorn-Seasoned Salt, page 156
Pizza seasoning spice or other seasoned salt

Wrap tofu in plastic wrap; seal. Overwrap in foil or place in a heavy plastic bag, pressing out all air. Freeze until firm or until ready to prepare. Freezing the tofu gives it a bread-like texture. Unwrap tofu and place on a plate; thaw completely. Preheat oven to 250F (120C). Cut tofu into 1/2-inch cubes; place on a baking sheet, spreading evenly in 1 layer. Season with Chinese Five-Spice Powder, garlic salt or other seasonings, as desired. Bake 2-1/2 to 3 hours or until tofu is dry, crisp and lightly browned. Stir occasionally with a spatula. Turn oven heat off. Let croutons stand in oven 30 minutes. Pack in an airtight container, then store at room temperature. Makes about 3 cups.

About 14 calories per 1/4 cup.

Japanese-Style Stock

A Japanese soup stock, excellent to use when stir-frying or to serve as a clear soup.

5 cups water
1 thick onion slice
1 celery stalk, sliced
1/2 cup mushroom stems or pieces, if desired

**1/4 cup mirin, medium-dry sherry
   or dry sherry**
1 envelope dashi-no-moto powder

Pour water into a saucepan over high heat; add onion, celery and mushrooms, if desired. Bring to a boil; add mirin or sherry. Reduce heat and simmer about 1 hour or until reduced to about 4 cups. Strain into a bowl, discarding solids. Stir in dashi-no-moto powder until dissolved. Makes about 2-1/2 cups.

About 35 calories per 1 cup.

Dashi-no-moto powder is an instant granular stock, based on the authentic dashi that is soup stock made from dried fish and sea vegetables.

Beef Broth

This rich, flavorful broth can be made ahead, then frozen for later use.

4 to 5 lbs. meaty beef or veal bones,
  preferably 1/2 of each
1 tablespoon peanut oil or vegetable oil
2 large onions, chopped
2 large carrots, sliced
1 celery stalk, sliced
1 cup celery leaves
1 cup mushrooms or mushroom stems
1 pig's foot, if desired

1 garlic clove, crushed
3 parsley sprigs
1/2 teaspoon dried leaf thyme
1/2 teaspoon dried leaf marjoram
1 bay leaf
1 tablespoon salt
8 black peppercorns
4 to 5 qts. water

Preheat oven to 350F (175C). Arrange bones in a shallow baking pan; bake 1 hour or until well browned, turning occasionally. Place wok over low heat; add oil. When hot, add onions, carrots, celery, celery leaves and mushrooms. Cook, stirring occasionally, 20 minutes or until vegetables are soft and slightly browned. Place browned bones, cooked vegetables and pig's foot, if desired, in a large stock pot. Add garlic, parsley, thyme, marjoram, bay leaf, salt, peppercorns and sufficient water to cover by about 1 inch. Bring to a boil; skim foam from surface until surface is clear. Reduce heat and simmer, partially covered, about 4 hours. Remove from heat; cool slightly. Strain into a large bowl, discarding bones and solids. Refrigerate until fat solidifies on top. Remove and discard fat. Pour broth into small containers; tightly cover. Refrigerate 2 to 3 days or freeze 3 to 4 months. Bring broth to a boil before using. Makes about 2-1/2 quarts.

About 12 calories per 1 cup.

Vegetable Broth

A nourishing, flavorful broth, ideal to serve for a light lunch or mid-afternoon beverage.

3 celery stalks, diced
2 onions, halved, each 1/2 studded with
  a whole clove
1 potato, thickly sliced
2 large carrots, sliced
About 1 cup mushroom stems

2 or 3 large parsley sprigs
1 bay leaf
4 or 5 black peppercorns
2 garlic cloves, if desired
About 3 qts. water
Salt

Combine all ingredients except salt in a stock pot; cover with water. Bring to a full boil. Reduce heat and simmer, uncovered, 1 to 2 hours. Remove from heat; cool slightly. Strain into a large bowl, discarding solids. Season to taste with salt. Pour broth into small containers; tightly cover. Refrigerate 2 to 3 days or freeze 3 to 4 months. Bring broth to a boil before using. Makes 4 to 6 cups.

About 4 calories per 1 cup.

How to Make Chicken Broth

1/Combine ingredients in a wok or saucepan. Bring to a boil; reduce heat and simmer.

2/Broth may be frozen in divided ice trays. Store cubes in a plastic bag in freezer to use as needed.

Chicken Broth

After making the broth, you have the bonus of poached chicken to use in salads or other recipes.

1 (3- to 3-1/2-lb.) chicken, cut up
1 large carrot, sliced
1/4 lb. mushrooms, chopped
2 shallots, minced
1 leek, white part only, chopped
1 small celery stalk

1-1/2 cups dry white wine
1 small garlic clove, if desired
2 to 3 qts. cold water
1 onion, peeled, studded with a whole clove
Salt

In a large wok, combine chicken, carrot, mushrooms, shallots, leek, celery, white wine and garlic, if desired. Bring to a full boil; boil 10 minutes. Skim foam from surface until surface is clear. Add sufficient water to cover chicken and vegetables. Add onion; reduce heat and simmer, partially covered, 20 to 30 minutes or until chicken is tender. Remove chicken pieces; let stand until cool enough to handle. Pull off and discard skin. Remove meat in large pieces; place in a large bowl. Spoon a little broth over chicken. Cover and refrigerate or freeze for future use. Return chicken bones to broth. Simmer 1 hour or until liquid is reduced by about 1/2. Remove from heat; cool slightly. Strain into a large bowl, discarding vegetables and bones. Refrigerate until fat solidifies on top. Remove and discard fat. Pour broth into small containers; tightly cover. Refrigerate 2 to 3 days or freeze 3 to 4 months. Bring broth to a boil before using. Makes about 1-1/2 quarts.

About 50 calories per 1 cup.

Fresh Tomato Sauce

A perfect sauce to make when you have an abundance of ripe tomatoes.

8 large tomatoes, about 3 lbs.
1 teaspoon peanut oil or vegetable oil
1/4 cup finely chopped onion
1/2 cup chopped green bell pepper
1/2 cup thinly sliced celery
1 teaspoon minced garlic, if desired
1-1/2 teaspoons chopped fresh basil or
  1/2 teaspoon dried leaf basil

1/8 teaspoon dried leaf thyme
1/8 teaspoon dried rosemary
1/8 teaspoon dried leaf oregano
Salt
Freshly ground black pepper

Bring a small saucepan of water to a boil. Plunge each tomato into boiling water 10 to 15 seconds. Hold each tomato under cold running water and peel off skin. Coarsely chop tomatoes, reserving juice. Place wok over high heat; add oil. When hot, add onion, bell pepper and celery; stir-fry 1 minute or until crisp-tender. Add garlic, if desired; stir-fry 30 seconds. Stir in tomatoes with juice and herbs. Continue to stir, breaking up tomatoes, until mixture is reduced to a thick, chunky sauce. Season to taste with salt and black pepper. Use immediately or ladle sauce into small containers; tightly cover. Refrigerate or freeze up to 3 months until ready to use. Makes about 2-1/2 cups.

About 160 calories per 1 cup.

Quick Tomato Sauce

A great sauce to make when time is of the essence.

2 teaspoons peanut oil or vegetable oil
1 large onion, chopped
1 garlic clove, minced
1 (28-oz.) can crushed tomatoes with
  puree or 1 (28-oz.) can Italian-style
  peeled tomatoes and
  1 tablespoon tomato paste

1 teaspoon Italian Seasoning, opposite
1/2 teaspoon salt
1/2 teaspoon sugar
2 teaspoons balsamic vinegar or
  other mild vinegar

Place wok over high heat; add oil. When hot, add onion; stir-fry 1 minute or until crisp-tender. Stir in garlic; stir-fry 30 seconds or until softened. Stir in tomatoes and tomato paste. Continue to stir, breaking up tomatoes until mixture is reduced to a thick, chunky sauce. Stir in herbs, salt, sugar and vinegar. Reduce heat; simmer 30 minutes, stirring occasionally. Use immediately or ladle sauce into small containers; tightly cover. Refrigerate or freeze up to 3 months until ready to use. Makes about 1 quart.

About 80 calories per 1 cup.

Italian Seasoning

A convenient seasoning mixture to have on hand.

3 tablespoons dried leaf basil   1 teaspoon onion powder
1 tablespoon dried leaf oregano   1 teaspoon garlic powder
1 tablespoon dried leaf marjoram

In a small jar, combine all ingredients; cover tightly. Shake to blend mixture. Store with your other spices in a cool, dark place. Makes about 1/3 cup.

About 4 calories per 1 teaspoon.

Quatre Epices

Although the French translation means "four spices," the mixture may contain five or more spices.

4 tablespoons freshly ground black pepper   1 teaspoon dry mustard
1 tablespoon ground ginger   1 teaspoon ground cloves
1 tablespoon freshly ground nutmeg

Combine ingredients in a food processor fitted with a metal blade; process until finely ground and well blended. Store in an airtight jar. Makes about 1/2 cup.

About 6 calories per 1 teaspoon.

A teaspoon of Quatre Epices equals 1/2 teaspoon black pepper, 1/8 teaspoon ground ginger, 1/8 teaspoon ground nutmeg and a pinch each of dry mustard and ground cloves.

Szechuan-Peppercorn-Seasoned Salt

For positively exotic flavor, use this seasoned salt rather than regular salt and pepper.

6 tablespoons kosher salt   **2 tablespoons Szechuan peppercorns**

Place dry wok over low heat; add salt and peppercorns. Stir until salt is lightly browned and peppercorns begin to smoke. Remove from heat; cool. Pour mixture into a food processor fitted with a metal blade; process at high speed 30 seconds. Or, crush mixture with a mortar and pestle. Store in a small jar with a tight-fitting lid. Makes about 1/2 cup.

About 2 calories per 1 teaspoon.

Szechuan peppercorns are dried reddish berries, resembling small flowers. They are fragrant and mildly hot.

Chinese Five-Spice Powder

Star anise are small, firm, star-shaped seed pods with a licorice flavor.

1 tablespoon Szechuan peppercorns   **1 tablespoon fennel seeds**
1/2 teaspoon ground cloves   **4 whole star anise**
1 tablespoon ground cinnamon

Place ingredients in a food processor fitted with a metal blade; process until finely ground and blended. Or, crush mixture with a mortar and pestle. Store in an airtight jar. Makes about 1/4 cup.

About 2 calories per 1 teaspoon.

Use Five-Spice Powder sparingly because it is very piquant.

Metric Chart

Comparison to Metric Measure

When You Know	Symbol	Multiply By	To Find	Symbol
teaspoons	tsp	5.0	milliliters	ml
tablespoons	tbsp	15.0	milliliters	ml
fluid ounces	fl. oz.	30.0	milliliters	ml
cups	c	0.24	liters	l
pints	pt.	0.47	liters	l
quarts	qt.	0.95	liters	l
ounces	oz.	28.0	grams	g
pounds	lb.	0.45	kilograms	kg
Fahrenheit	F	5/9 (after subtracting 32)	Celsius	C

Liquid Measure to Milliliters

1/4 teaspoon	=	1.25 milliliters
1/2 teaspoon	=	2.5 milliliters
3/4 teaspoon	=	3.75 milliliters
1 teaspoon	=	5.0 milliliters
1-1/4 teaspoons	=	6.25 milliliters
1-1/2 teaspoons	=	7.5 milliliters
1-3/4 teaspoons	=	8.75 milliliters
2 teaspoons	=	10.0 milliliters
1 tablespoon	=	15.0 milliliters
2 tablespoons	=	30.0 milliliters

Fahrenheit to Celsius

F	C
200—205	95
220—225	105
245—250	120
275	135
300—305	150
325—330	165
345—350	175
370—375	190
400—405	205
425—430	220
445—450	230
470—475	245
500	260

Liquid Measure to Liters

1/4 cup	=	0.06 liters
1/2 cup	=	0.12 liters
3/4 cup	=	0.18 liters
1 cup	=	0.24 liters
1-1/4 cups	=	0.3 liters
1-1/2 cups	=	0.36 liters
2 cups	=	0.48 liters
2-1/2 cups	=	0.6 liters
3 cups	=	0.72 liters
3-1/2 cups	=	0.84 liters
4 cups	=	0.96 liters
4-1/2 cups	=	1.08 liters
5 cups	=	1.2 liters
5-1/2 cups	=	1.32 liters

INDEX